Praise for *Never to Surrender!*

"Horrendous prison conditions have long been conveniently ignored by U.S. lawmakers. The abusive use of solitary confinement, however, has at least begun to be acknowledged and is sparking efforts at legislative reform. Such campaigns will receive a major boost from *Never to Surrender!* Mr. De Palma tells a remarkable story of suffering but also of resilience. His book is powerful evidence that long-term isolation is torture—a torture that not only hurts the victim, but also calls into question our belief in ourselves as a moral and just society."

—**Juan E. Mendez**, Professor of Human Rights in Residence, Washington College of Law, and Former United Nations Special Rapporteur on Torture (2010–2016)

"The day Dr. Martin Luther King Jr. was killed, sanitation workers marching in Memphis carried signs that said, 'I am a man.' Frank De Palma is a man. A man who was treated like an animal, forced to endure the worst form of torture: isolation. Frank De Palma languished in solitary confinement for 22 years and 36 days in a prison not in some far away land, but right here in the United States. Across those 22 years he battled for his brain, for his sanity, for his life, for human connection. His is a story of tragedy but also of the fierceness of the human spirit."

—**Angela Hattery, Ph.D.**, Professor, University of Delaware, and coauthor of *Way Down in the Hole: Race, Intimacy, and the Reproduction of Racial Ideologies in Solitary Confinement*

"In a 'life or death and no in-between' prison, with constant violence and threats of rape, a man has to fight, be enslaved or die. Frank De Palma's grit permitted him to survive the fights only to be punished with 22 years of solitary confinement. His toughness and integrity earned him the respect of prison gladiators and guards alike, and now, free at last, he provides a thrilling and seamlessly vibrant account of the entire ordeal, including lessons from 'Inside' that offer invaluable wisdom about our human condition."

—**Terry A. Kupers, M.D., M.S.P.,** author of *Prison Madness* and *Solitary: The Inside Story of Supermax Isolation*

"Never to Surrender! is a gut-wrenching tale where solitary confinement is used to torture and destroy what is left in a person who is trying to survive prison—and the people who run it."

—**Karen Gedney, M.D.,** author of *30 Years Behind Bars: Trials of a Prison Doctor*

"Frank De Palma's new book is a *tour de force*. Frank's ability to share his story is almost seamless and simply amazing. Like many books from ex-convicts who have been lucky enough to survive prison—let alone solitary confinement—*Never to Surrender! 22 Years in Solitary, The Battle for My Soul in a U. S. Prison* takes us inside; inside of what those 22 years and 36 days really were like. HELL! Highly recommend; a must-read!"

—**Earl Smith, Ph.D.,** Professor, University of Delaware, and coauthor of *Way Down in the Hole: Race, Intimacy, and the Reproduction of Racial Ideologies in Solitary Confinement*

NEVER TO SURRENDER!

22 YEARS IN SOLITARY

The Battle for My Soul in a U.S. Prison

FRANK DE PALMA
WITH MARY BUSER

Published by:
Homelawn Publishing
BROOKLYN, NY

Copyright © 2024 Frank De Palma and Mary Buser

ISBNs:
979-8-9903553-0-9 (paperback)
979-8-9903553-1-6 (hardcover)
979-8-9903553-2-3 (ebook)

Cover design: Zarah Zurita
Interior layout: Gary A. Rosenberg

"Never to Surrender"

A Poem by Frank De Palma
(written in April 2017, a year and a half
before his release from prison)

*In my life, I have experienced much of the ugliness that I
believe is borne of evil itself. The fear I felt slowly turned to
bitterness, then to resentment, next to anger, which gave way
to hate—only to become a consuming rage that finally erupted
in violence.*

*Hatred is a poison to the mind, the heart, and ultimately to
the soul. To begin the victim, only to become the predator and
to look upon most as prey; it fills me with a pain and sorrow
that words could never convey.*

*I lost my youth, my family, and friends. I lost my hopes
and dreams, even my memories began to fade. How could it
happen? Why did it happen? For I do not understand even to
this very day.*

*I was not born to hurt or kill, yet it became my way; why,
when so young, I was filled with promise and hope; why, when
but for a moment I lost my way . . . to hold my friend as his life
slipped away. Why was I charged with so heavy a punishment
when I but spoke my heart . . . from the promise and hope I
held, did your black-robed decree take from me.*

*Through the years I fought, and I survived, not knowing
that something inside me had died. I surrendered all, including
my will, to some void that became my world; a place where*

emptiness became my peace and nothingness my only embrace. With nothing more to think, nothing more to say, I closed my door and quietly slipped away.

In the years that passed I did not protest, nor did I resist, for gone from the ugliness and loss, I had entered my inner abyss. It is a sorrowful time that I will sometimes recall, though only to remind me of the horrors that exist lest I lose my way.

My spirit rose up and rejected the death I had chosen to be, to rise up and fight for my mind, my heart, and my soul. There can be no surrender to the ugliness borne of evil, for to do so is to die a death that even death itself does fear. I have rediscovered the promise and hope in me, and even unto my death to this world, my spirit shall ever be free.

Contents

PART TWO

PART THREE

Foreword

I have read many books about prison, high and low art that try to fathom the darkness that is confinement, but rarely have I read such an engaging portrait of a life inside, broken slowly by the never-ending death that is prison. *Never to Surrender!* is a potent narrative that will not lie down. Indeed, it is a miracle that Frank De Palma is alive to tell his story, having spent so much time in solitary. What you learn from reading this chronicle is that man can be cruel beyond measure and that a child born into the world without love bears those scars for life.

I taught in the prison where Frank De Palma did the last of his time and the associate warden who literally saved him was one of the few people inside who did everything she could to help people like him. She thought of prison not as a death sentence but as a possibility of another life. I was heartened to learn of her extraordinary efforts in preparing Frank to live outside again.

What also startled me was how these narratives are perpetrated by administrators who find themselves in charge of people who got snared in the law's net. The drugging of inmates to "calm" them, the purposeful withholding of food and blankets, the intentional darkness for days, the blinding sun that follows, the taciturn agreements with guards "who let things happen," and no one knows why. This is commonplace in prison, a trope really, but it was no less painful to read of it even as I have witnessed it in my thirty years of volunteering.

Most people think of prison as a necessary evil—or worse, just don't think of it. Beyond a cage, it is a literal stopping point in a life, a place where all rules go away and, in turn, everyone is suspect. Fear is the common denominator and power its bludgeon. Sadly, all too sadly, the guards become pawns in the game and before long they are struggling to survive the slow ebb of their humanity. Not all, but many persist in dreaming of a state retirement after looking the other way for their time inside.

Frank De Palma's book is a chilling recognition of prison's depravity and an almost unbelievable story of survival. How he lived to write this I cannot say; that it unfolds with excruciating precision, the years slowly dribbling out like pain from a needle, the sorry prison complex that lives in eternal hope of being fixed, and the families that wait and wait for all of this to change—this is the methodical killing field he rose from to tell his story.

—Shaun T. Griffin,
Poet and Activist

PART ONE

*There is nothing concealed that will not be disclosed
or hidden that will not be made known . . .*
—Luke 12:2

CHAPTER 1

Nevada State Prison

Congratulations, you are now one of us, perhaps.
Go out there and live or die.

—Zeke, the old intake prisoner
at the Nevada State Prison

At approximately 1 a.m., the morning after I had been sentenced to serve ten years in the Nevada State Prison for grand theft auto, I was awakened by a couple of jailers who ordered me to grab any personal belongings, limited to legal documents, and to exit the cell. I complied and was handcuffed and taken by elevator down to the third floor of what was then Las Vegas's Clark County Jail.

On the way down, a jailer chuckled that I was lucky, as I was being driven solo, in a van, to the prison and should be thankful because a van was a luxury compared to the crowded transport wagon that was normally used.

I was taken to a holding cell where I was ordered to strip naked, then told to reveal my body parts for inspection to ensure I had no hidden weapons or tools that might aid me in escaping custody. Too scared to protest the humiliating ordeal, I did as I was told. When complete, I was handed a set of orange transport overalls several sizes too big for my five-foot-six-inch frame.

With my wavy reddish-brown hair pulled into a ponytail, I

looked like any other eighteen-year-old in the mid-1970s, save for the splash of freckles across my nose that had not yet faded. Once dressed, I put on some loafers and was fitted with belly chains, wrist restraints, and leg shackles and escorted to the elevator, where we rode down to the lower level of the jail's garage. I was met with a blast of cold air and started shivering as I was helped into the van. A few minutes later, we began the six-hour drive from Las Vegas to Carson City, where the maximum-security prison was located.

As we drove, I wondered what awaited me. The night before, several other inmates at the jail had told me stories about the Nevada State Prison and offered advice about what to do once I got there. An original advisory was, "Find the biggest, meanest convict there, go up to him, and punch him in the face. That'll let everyone know you're not to be messed with." Someone else warned me not to do that unless I was trying to get killed. Of all the things I was told, there was one constant theme—that of violence, of murders, riots, and stabbings inside the maximum-security prison. I hoped it was a lot of hype and exaggeration.

For hours we drove, stopping only once for a bathroom break. The driver and his buddy ordered themselves some burgers and fries, but none for me. I said nothing. Slowly, the sky began to lighten as a new day dawned on the horizon. I couldn't help but notice how majestic the sunrise looked and realized, quite intimately, how we all take so much for granted, especially our families, our loved ones, our freedoms. We go about our daily routines as though nothing could ever disturb our way of life. A month earlier, I had been camping in the mountains.

We drove on and passed through some tiny little towns with nothing more than a few shops, a gas station, a saloon, a diner, and scattered, well-weathered houses. The West in its purest state. We finally drove through a large town of sorts. The guard yelled that we were almost to my new home and that it was "pretty."

When the prison came into view, my stomach lurched. The whitish-gray and brownstone brick structure looked like one of those castle dungeons in some gothic lore coming into view through a murky mist—only I saw it very clearly and it was real. I felt a sense of complete hopelessness and a foreboding fear and dread like I'd never known. I wanted to cry and almost did but somehow held it back. The guard must have seen the look on my face because he laughed and said, "You think that's ugly, wait'll you get inside."

We drove into the parking lot and up to the tower gate, where a guard wearing mirrored sunglasses and holding a high-powered rifle leaned out. He waved us in, and we came to a stop. I was handed off to two guards who took the chains off me, placed me in handcuffs, and silently took me to a drab area used for processing incoming prisoners. Convicts milled about the place. They looked cold, hard, and dangerous, with their face and neck tattoos and muscled physiques. My sense of dread grew, but I forced myself to look composed. There were also a few yawning guards overseeing things.

The convicts were doing all the incoming inmate processing. A guard removed my handcuffs and told me to sit on a bench until one of the convicts called me up. As I sat there, I found myself asking God to keep me safe. Funny how certain situations tend to make a person want to get close to God. Well, after eighteen years of not praying, I quickly became one of those people.

Someone said, "Zeke, let's do this fish, so we can get back to biz."

The one processing me was Zeke. He motioned me over. At the desk, I answered some simple questions, like my name, date of birth, and where I was born. It took less than ten minutes.

Then this Zeke guy stamped my processing card with a red timestamp—9:17 a.m. His next words, I will never forget: "Congratulations, you are now one of us, perhaps. Go out there and live or die."

I was moved into a small cell in a section they called the "Fish Tank" where the new "fish" were held. The cell was so small that my outstretched fingertips could brush the walls on either side of me. The cracked porcelain toilet looked like something from the turn of the twentieth century. The cell had a 40-watt light bulb with a little chain that I pulled to turn the light on and off. Cockroaches ran up the walls, and I shuddered at the sight of them. The Brooklyn projects back in New York where I had grown up had been infested with cockroaches, and I couldn't stand them.

As I sat wondering what would come next, I began to cry, and even at that very beginning, my tears felt wrong and out of place. I knew any crying would have to stop, but not right then, as I couldn't keep my tears from flowing. There I was, just a few months shy of my nineteenth birthday, in a maximum-security prison filled with ruthless criminals. I couldn't understand what had gone so wrong in my life to bring me to this place that felt so far away from everything that was human and normal.

That afternoon, a convict brought me a big steel tray piled with food and gave me a metal cup.

"Thank you," I said, "but I'm not hungry."

"I don't give a fuck," he said, and left.

The guard told me someone would pick it up later. I pushed the tray aside and laid down on an old wood-frame bed, its worn mattress sagging badly in the middle. With leather straps instead of springs, it looked and felt ancient. I covered myself with the itchy blanket that was given to me and spent the night praying to God and whispering to my mom. Somewhere along the way, exhaustion overcame me, and I fell asleep.

CHAPTER 2

A Good Boy

My name is Frank De Palma. I was born on May 28, 1956, in Brooklyn, New York, worlds away from the Nevada State Prison and all its misery. I grew up not too far from the salt air of Coney Island and its famous roller coaster, the Cyclone. I can forever see myself running down the boardwalk on summer afternoons. How I loved that boardwalk! I was especially drawn to the wooden slats and the way they all came together so neatly. Dad said I would have made a good carpenter. Oh, what might have been!

There was plenty for a boy to do in Brooklyn in the early sixties, lots of open fields for exploration. As young as six years old, I used to run up to the train tracks, hop a fence, and cross over. I was especially intrigued by a thickly wooded area on the other side of the tracks.

Combing through the brush one afternoon, I stumbled upon what must have been a slaughterhouse. I slipped inside and came upon crates that were stacked on top of each other. Panicked sounds were coming from inside them. I ventured closer and saw feathers sticking out, and then I saw all these poor chickens packed in tight. I felt so bad for them. I put my fingers through the wire so I could pet them, talk to them, try to make them feel a little better. I told them I was sorry they were crammed in there like that, but that they should try to get along now. I told them I loved them. All they did was peck my fingers. But I like to think they heard me.

I always felt a deep connection to animals, and I tried to get out to visit the chickens as much as I could. But one afternoon a frightening incident put an end to my carefree wanderings. I was heading home, crossing back over the train tracks, when I slipped and fell. I scrambled to get up, but my shirt had gotten snagged on a bolt in one of the rails. I tried to yank it loose, but it wouldn't give. I looked up and sure enough, a train was coming, its headlights bearing down on me. I ripped the shirt off my back as fast as I could and stumbled to the other side of the tracks as the train whooshed by. I never crossed those tracks again.

The streets of my section of Brooklyn were lined with bungalow houses filed neatly next to one another, filled with what I imagined to be happy, little families. I only wished it was a happy family that dwelled inside my home. I lived in an apartment in the projects with my mother, father, and sister, Marie, who was three years older.

My mom was my heaven. A petite woman, not even five feet tall, she was always ready with a quick smile, a gentle touch, a warm hug. Her name was Mary O'Hagan before she married my dad. An intelligent woman, Mom worked the graveyard shift over in Manhattan as a proofreader. She was once named "Proofreader of the Year" at the Wall Street bank where she worked. I was very proud of that. Still am.

My mom also happened to be deaf, the result of spinal meningitis and double pneumonia in her infancy. But her handicap was something I barely noticed. She called me "Fwankie," and when she said she was cooking "spinenni," I knew we were having spaghetti for dinner. My mother's voice was a comfort to me, not odd at all. One time, a friend I walked home from school with started to mimic my mother and I punched him, knocking him to the ground. If the way she spoke sounded odd to others, it was beautiful to me, and anyone who dared make fun of her got a punch in the face—automatic.

My mother and I were connected beyond words. She was an expert lip reader, and we relied on some crude hand gestures to communicate, since my dad forbade us from learning sign language, which he viewed as a concession to her handicap. There were to be no concessions. But it didn't matter. My mom and I understood each other anyway, always in sync. She was my loving refuge—safe, affectionate, and doting. My father, on the other hand, was my hell. That's how I came to think of them. Heaven and hell. My father, Anthony De Palma, was the most dominating force in my life. A compact yet strong man with reddish-brown hair, he spoke his mind and exerted his will, often with his fists. I both loved and hated him but always feared him in the worst way. His temper, his rage, was so palpable, so intense and frightening, that I cannot recall ever fearing anything in my life like I feared my dad—not even a death threat from the Aryan Warriors, or an M14 pointed at my head by prison guards. Nothing was as terrifying to me as my father.

I have to say he was a good man in that he always provided for his family. He had a part-time truck route, and between that and patching together odd jobs, we never went without. But he was also insanely violent, his rage often directed at my poor mother. I watched helplessly as he beat her savagely with his fists. Sometimes he would throw something heavy at her with such force it would knock her to the floor. I often saw blood streaming down her face, an image that pains me to this day. Being a little kid, all I could do was stand in the corner and cry. I hated him and wanted to kill him for hurting my mom. There were moments when I couldn't stand it anymore, and I would rush him, a child yelling at a grown man to leave his mother alone. This only enraged him further, and I'd get picked up and, like a projectile, I'd be slammed into the wall.

Every day of my childhood, I went to bed in fear, and I woke up in fear. Anything could set this man off, and it wasn't just my mother he targeted. He would also come after Marie and me, using a belt or his hands on us. Getting hit as much as I did, I started getting used to it and didn't mind it nearly as much as it pained me to see my mom and sister being brutalized by him. I just wasn't big enough to stop him. I felt so helpless.

But one day, I made a discovery that gave me a little power. Just as he was about to go after my mom, I accidentally knocked something over and broke it. He whirled around and came at me instead. In that instant, I realized that there was actually something I could do. Since I was able to tell when he was about to have one of his moments, I would knock something over or mouth off, and he would turn his rage on me. I would get the beatings and not my mother and sister. So really, becoming the diversion was my way to protect them, and that made me feel good and a little proud of myself. It also made me feel less afraid. Marie knew exactly what I was doing, but neither of us said anything about it.

When I was nine years old, my parents divorced, and my mom moved out. Marie and I stayed with my father because my mom couldn't afford to take us with her. I remember Mom crying hard when she hugged us before she left. We all cried.

Mom moved not too far away to an apartment in Bay Ridge, not far from the Verrazzano-Narrows Bridge, and we would spend weekends with her. That's when Mom and I became very close, especially when my sister didn't come for whatever reason. Probably girly stuff. When Mom and I were by ourselves, she would talk to me about things she didn't discuss when Marie was there. She would pat my head and tell me I would meet a nice girl one day and that we would be happy together and that she knew I would never hit a woman. I had already made that decision myself; there was no way I would be like my father in that regard. She also told me that my dad wasn't a bad man, just a war-beaten broken man.

I loved the one-on-one attention my mother gave me when Marie wasn't around. I felt I could be more myself, too, not embarrassed by the closeness I wanted to have with my mother. In the evenings, when I was drowsy and falling asleep, I would hear the tugboats out on the river. Their long bellowing sounds seemed to call to me, comforting me, and with my mom sleeping soundly nearby, I felt safe. I wished I could have stayed there forever.

Back at home with my dad, I walked on eggshells. My father did not tolerate failure on any level. Any perceived failure by me, his only son, was met with severe physical and psychological punishment. Things got especially tense when it came to my schoolwork. If I made a mistake reciting my multiplication tables, he'd give me a look that shot fear through my heart. I would freeze up, which of course, meant more mistakes, leading to a verbal belittling—"Stupid! Dummy! Worthless!"—followed by a sharp slap to the face, causing yet another bloody nose. But it was always the words that hurt the most.

School was just several city blocks from where I lived, but a city block in New York is long. As a child, my forays from home to school and back were grand adventures. But by the time I turned eleven, I was of the age that made me a target for bullies and street gangs. I was not a bully, nor did I belong to any gang.

My father made it clear that only cowards joined gangs. "I'd rather see you dead than part of some gang of cowardly dogs," he'd rant. "Real men stand alone and fight their own battles and do whatever is necessary to protect their families and loved ones."

I obeyed the part about not joining a gang, but not the part about standing and fighting. I found it much less painful to run when I was confronted by neighborhood thugs demanding whatever change I had in my pockets. I did quite a bit of running in those early days. But that would change. Just shy of my twelfth birthday, I was walking home from school one afternoon when someone hollered at me, "Run for your life or die!"

Fear welled up inside me. I turned around and saw one of the local hoods wearing his black leather jacket fitted with shiny silver studs. I recognized him as one of the Shamrocks. I especially hated them because I'm half Irish, and they still liked to hurt other Irish kids.

He sauntered closer, smirking, and I took off. But he was right behind me, taunting, "Hey scaredy-cat, run faster—that's it, faster!"

I hated this. I hated being afraid, of living with fear, and of being in fear every single day of my life. Something began welling up inside me. It was not fear, but something else, something stronger, and as I ran, it grew and grew, and I just wanted to crush—to kill—everything and everybody who wanted to hurt my mom, my sister, and me. I wanted to crush it all away, all my fear and all that made me afraid. In what would be the defining moment of my life, I stopped running. Never again would I run from anyone or anything. I turned to face him.

The Shamrock thug pointed his finger at me. "Did I tell you to stop? Maybe you didn't hear me. Let me repeat myself. Keep running or I'll kill you."

I ran, all right, but I ran right at him. I felt fear, anger, desperation, rage, and maybe even hatred all at once, and it came together and exploded like a bomb. I was the bomb, and I exploded as my body slammed into his. We both went to the ground hard. I was crying, and at the same time yelling at him. "You're going to kill me? No, I'm going to kill you!"

We fell down a short set of concrete steps into a garbage alley, where a glass bottle was rolling around. We both reached for it. I got it. I hit him in the head with it until the bottle broke. I stood up and kicked him and kept kicking him until I fell down. My leg just went out. I got up and saw all this blood on my pants and shoes. The guy's face was all bloody, and he wasn't moving. I ran back up the steps and raced home, afraid someone might see me because I thought I'd killed him.

I snuck quietly into the apartment and changed my clothes. I carefully washed my shoes and threw my pants down the garbage chute. The next day in school, I heard about how someone beat up this kid really bad and that he had to go to the hospital. I asked if he was dying and was told no but that there was a crazy kid killer on the loose. I was so relieved.

As things heated up on the streets, my dad was tutoring me in warfare, pounding home his main theme: Never join a gang. Gangs were for cowards! Looking back, I have to say that my life would have been a lot easier if I *had* joined a gang. But no, I would fight my own battles, and as the street rumbles continued, no matter how afraid I was, I never ran away. I also learned never to hesitate when the moment called for action. Dad had been on the frontlines in Korea and said that hesitation in battle could end in death and possibly the deaths of those one is responsible for. I took what he said to heart. I so wanted my father to be proud of me.

I was turning into a decent street fighter, but despite this, one afternoon, I was no match for four local hoods. Without warning, I was surrounded by them. "What are you doing on our turf?" they demanded.

Before I could protest that this was the street where I lived, they had me on the ground. All four of them went at me, kicking me with their boots, fists raining down hard punches all over my body. I shielded myself as best I could, but it was useless. After a few final kicks to my ribs, they turned and left me there. I lay still for a long while before I was able to pick myself up and limp home. My clothes were torn, I could barely see out of my left eye, and every last bit of me hurt. Looking as bad as I felt, I hobbled in the front door.

My dad looked me over and asked, "What does the other guy look like?"

I explained that there wasn't just one guy—that there had been four of them and that I had fought my best, but I still got beat up.

He rose from his chair. "Get out of my house!"

"But, Dad—"

"I don't care if there were ten of them. You don't set foot in here again till you get each and every one of them. You understand?"

"Okay, Dad."

I left the apartment and gimped back out to the street. Just twelve years old, I had no idea what to do or where to go. I made my way into an apartment building foyer, where there were a couple of old stuffed chairs. No one seemed to notice me, so I curled up in one of the chairs and fell asleep.

When I woke up, dawn was breaking, and I was hungry. I had to figure things out. Before I was going to beat anybody up, I figured I should eat something. I knew the neighborhood well, and I walked up to the main avenue, watching as delivery trucks pulled up at the doors of still darkened bakeries and delicatessens, laying out crates of milk, bread, and pastries. I noticed the drivers put a little bit of food to one side. It looked tempting, but I held back and was glad I did. The local hobos were just rousing, emerging from alleyways and empty buildings, and they moved right in on the food.

Even though I was a kid, had I touched it, I would have gotten hurt badly by them. Unlike regular down-and-out bums, the hobos were scary. They often rode railway cars and were dangerous if confronted. People knew to avoid them. But after they were gone and the coast was clear, I snatched what was left. Surviving the streets was doable. You just had to follow the unwritten rules.

After my belly was full, I turned my attention to my ripped and bloodied clothes. I looked up at the clotheslines that criss-crossed between the apartment buildings, hopped a wall, and grabbed on to the bottoms of a pair of jeans and snatched myself a newly laundered tee shirt.

Next was hunting down my prey. It took me close to ten days, but one by one, I got all four of them. I didn't exactly fight fair as I used a variety of objects as weapons—a bat-sized chunk of wood, a liter-sized bottle, a garbage can lid. One kid I kicked in the face three times while he sat on the stoop outside his building. After each attack, I would run away in a hurry. My worst fear was that my father would beat me for using weapons on all but one of them, but I was doing the best I could.

It wasn't till years later that I realized that never, not even one time, did I even think of lying to my father. I could have told him I took those guys two at a time with my bare hands, and he'd have been none the wiser. It just never occurred to me to lie.

On that tenth day, after I'd gotten them all, I headed home. When I walked through the front door, my father eyed me. "Well?

"I got them, Dad. I got all four of them."

I told him how it all went down, and how I'd also stolen food from the grocery market. He said that I only did what I had to do to survive, and no one could fault me for that. I nervously told him I'd used makeshift weapons.

"Good," he said. "Shows you're committed to victory over your enemies. You hungry?"

I nodded yes.

He made me a big deli-meat sandwich, then grabbed two glasses and split one of his beers with me. I felt like a conquering hero.

Marie looked at me and pinched her nose. "Frankie, you stink."

My dad laughed at that. After we ate, I took a bath and went to bed, the word "Good" repeating in my head. Though he rarely said it, on that day, my dad told me I was good. It was a golden moment.

Not long afterward, one of the neighborhood gang leaders approached me, arms outstretched, palms up. "Hey, Frankie, how you doin'? Listen, we're cool. We're cool now, okay?"

I nodded. No one ever bothered me again.

But I didn't have to worry about the bad streets of Brooklyn anymore, anyway. In 1970, when I was fourteen, my dad decided we were moving. He and his new wife, Wanda, and my sister, Marie, and I were headed for Las Vegas, Nevada. My dad had his sights set on a job at the casinos. Plus, I suffered from severe asthma, resulting in frequent trips to the emergency room. My dad thought drier air would be better for me. In some ways, he was a caring father. Soon, my mom and her new husband would also relocate to Las Vegas.

Nevada was sure different from Brooklyn. The first thing I remember was the sight of shimmering heat waves rising from the pavement. I'd never seen anything like that before, and I was mesmerized by it. Shortly after we arrived, I got my very own dog, a golden Lab puppy. I named him Bud, and he followed me everywhere. I just loved him. With Bud at my side, I was in good spirits as we settled into our new home. I was also feeling good, physically. The Nevada air was much drier than back East, and just like that, my lifelong bouts with asthma vanished.

But what did not vanish was my dad's violent streak. He beat Wanda just as he had beaten my mother. Business as usual. But shortly after I turned sixteen, it all came to an end. Once again, he'd flown into a rage and had Wanda cowering in a corner. To my utter surprise, I grabbed him and flung him out of the kitchen and into the living room, where he flipped backward over a table. He looked up at me from the floor, stunned.

A strength and anger rose up in me that I'd never known before. I pointed my finger at him. "You hit her again—you hit any one of us again—and I will kill you, you understand?"

He nodded.

The scared little boy was no more.

CHAPTER 3

An Impulsive Act
and a Hang-'Em-High Judge

It was just another warm, lazy evening in Las Vegas, and I was sitting out front, shooting the breeze with the neighbors and keeping an eye on Bud, who was running around the street with the other dogs. I was seventeen by now, and in the three years since I'd gotten Bud, we did everything together—hiking, fishing, camping up at Lee Canyon in the mountains north of Las Vegas. He was a great companion, and in one scary situation, he may even have saved my life.

We were out camping, and I was just getting the fire going, when I heard Bud growling. It was unlike Bud to growl, friendly fella that he was. But I looked up and froze. A mountain lion was looming over us, crouched on a ledge just a few feet away. Bud sprung up and charged him, and that cat turned and took off. Another time, a truckload of Mexicans pulled up in front of my house and piled out, one of them pointing a wooden bat at me. The previous day I'd gotten into a fight with some kid outside school, and I guess I got the better of him. The guy with the bat let me know it was his brother I'd beaten up. But before he could move on me, Bud charged him, teeth bared. The guy dropped the bat so fast, and they all jumped back in the truck and peeled out.

Bud was always so protective of me, sensing when I was in any type of danger. But it was more than that. Much more. He would also snuggle up to me when he knew I was feeling down.

For a bruised and kicked-around kid, Bud showed me a gentleness and warmth I wasn't used to. Bud was my best friend.

It seemed this element of gentleness and warmth had been inching its way into my teenage life, and it felt rather nice. As I kept my eye on Bud, I was thinking about my special girl. I had met her shortly after our move to Las Vegas. In a random encounter at the local park, I'd been leaning against a tree, smoking a joint, when she and her little dog came trotting along. She was Asian, slight in stature with long black hair. I thought she was pretty. She noticed me, too, and marched right up to me, demanding I put out the joint. "The smell is offensive, and it is affecting my dog!"

I smiled and snuffed it out. "Sure, no problem."

Satisfied that she'd resolved the situation, she harrumphed and continued on her way. But I followed after her. "Hey, mind if I tag along?"

She didn't exactly say yes, but then again, she didn't say no. I tried a little small talk without any luck. Then I told her about Bud, and the gates opened. She told me her name was Vivien, and that her parents had emigrated from China to the United States. I told her that I was originally from New York. Not quite as exotic, but hey! We chatted away, and it was all just so easy and natural. By the time we reached the end of the path, I was tucking her phone number into my pocket.

It was while I was daydreaming about an upcoming date with Vivien that I heard a revving engine, up on the hill. I stood up, irritated. The neighborhood jerk, who was always racing his pickup truck down the street, was at it again. Neighbors had called the cops on this kid more than once, but they said they couldn't do anything about it.

I could see the white pickup racing down the hill now and the dogs were scattering. But for some reason, Bud hadn't moved. I felt a flash of panic. "Bud!"

He looked up at me and our eyes locked. In an instant the truck was on him, running him over and speeding away.

I raced out to the road and knelt beside my dog. "Bud, Bud!" I patted his sweet head as he licked my hand. I pleaded with him through my tears. "No, no, Bud, my good boy. No!" But a moment later, his eyelids dropped, and he was gone.

Neighbors and friends were crowding around, trying to comfort me. I was inconsolable. I stood up and looked in the direction of the truck, my grief turning to cold rage. *He hadn't even hit the brakes. He hadn't swerved to avoid hitting Bud. And he never even stopped after he'd hit him. He just ran over my beloved dog and kept on going!*

I gathered Bud's lifeless body in my arms and gently laid it out in the front yard. And then I broke and ran.

I knew exactly where this guy lived. When I got to his house, I pounded on the front door. "Get out here, asshole! Get out here now so I can kick your ass!"

All was quiet inside. I kicked the door. "Get out here!"

Still nothing. But he was in there, all right, the coward. The truck that had just run over Bud was sitting in the driveway, the engine cooling off. I saw the keys dangling in the ignition. In an impulsive move, I jumped in, started it up, and backed it out into the street. I drove around the block, crazed with anger, grief, and all kinds of wild emotion. *You take away the best thing in my life? No!*

When I came back around, I had one thought: *You're not coming out? Okay, then I'm coming in.* I turned the wheel toward the house, hitting a curb that launched the truck into the air, crashing it through the front window. It was a hard collision, glass and drywall raining down everywhere, the windshield covered with wires and all manner of debris. The force of it threw me around the cab, and I blacked out.

When I came to, I was surrounded by police, their guns pointed at me. "Put your hands in plain sight."

I did as I was told.

I was arrested and spent a couple of weeks in the county jail before my dad was able to put together the money to bail me out. While I was in there, he buried Bud for me. I was charged with reckless driving, endangerment, destruction of personal property, and grand theft auto. As daunting as these charges were, a deal was worked out between the lawyers, and luckily for me, all the charges were dropped except for grand theft auto. If I pleaded guilty to that, I would get a ten-year suspended sentence with five years' probation after that. And after two and a half years of good behavior, I could petition the court to have my record expunged. Though crashing a truck through a house was a serious matter, thankfully, no one besides me had been hurt. The kid who'd killed Bud had been hiding outside in the bushes the whole time.

It was a good deal, everyone agreed. If all went according to plan, I would not be serving any prison time. My lawyer said we had a judge who was reasonable and would likely put his seal of approval on it in an upcoming court date.

It would be about a year before the legalities were worked out and everything would be finalized. Meantime, life went about as normally as possible with this legal matter hanging over my head. I was eighteen now and had dropped out of high school, mostly to spite my father. But I had a job, enabling me to buy my first car, a Chevy Impala. I worked as a limousine driver for a wedding outfit called Chapel of the Bells. I enjoyed my job, which was to drive the betrothed couple to the Las Vegas courthouse to pick up their marriage license, and then it was off to the chapel. I waited outside while they got married, and then I drove the newlyweds to wherever they wanted to go next. It wasn't anything great, but it paid for my outings with

Vivien, and it would tide me over while I figured out what I wanted to do with my life.

By now, Vivien and I had become inseparable. When I wasn't working and she wasn't busy finishing up her senior year in high school, we were together, hopping in my Impala, taking drives into the mountains, grabbing a burger, or just cuddling on the couch, watching a movie. And as my court date approached, we were looking forward to a special evening. I knew her parents by now, and they approved of me. But they were also very traditional and steeped in their native culture.

One evening, as Vivien and I were getting ready to go out, her mother pulled me aside and made an odd request: She asked that Vivien and I not have sex until she was eighteen. I was a little surprised, but they were from the old country, and I guess it was a cultural thing. I wasn't exactly thrilled, but I told her I would honor her wishes. I could see that Vivien was relieved and pleased, and that, of course, made me happy. But now, her eighteenth birthday was approaching, just one week after my court date. This would not only be Vivien's first time, but it would also be mine, and we both wanted it to be special. Vivien suggested we first go out to dinner at a nice restaurant. I liked the idea, too.

In the weeks leading up to my court appearance, my lawyer told me the judge I was to appear before had suffered a heart attack, and for the time being, his cases would be handled by another judge with a heavy-handed reputation. Despite this unsettling news, my lawyer still felt it should all go fine, especially as the district attorney was satisfied with the plea arrangement. I gave it little thought. I just wanted the whole thing over with.

Finally, the day came that I stood in a Las Vegas courtroom before Judge Paul Goldman, prepared to plead guilty to grand theft auto. The judge asked me if there was anything I wanted to say before he passed his sentence. This is where I was expected to say I was sorry for my actions.

"Yes, sir, there is," I said. "I am sorry any of this happened, yes, I am. But, your honor, I'm also sorry that my best friend is dead. And I'm sorry the person who killed him isn't here facing charges himself. Oh, I know the life of an animal and the life of a child isn't the same—it's apples and oranges. But it's still love, just the same, and Bud was my best friend. I loved him, your honor."

I spoke from my heart, unaware that people in the courtroom were looking at me and whispering, that my father was waving at me, and that my lawyer was nudging me to shut up.

The judge looked at me sternly. "That's enough," he said. "You don't sound sorry to me at all. I don't have to agree to this plea deal, and in fact, I'm not going to. We can go back to square one and put all the charges back on the table, or I can sentence you to prison on the grand theft auto."

I shrugged, as only a cocky eighteen-year-old would. "Do what you have to do."

"Fine, I will," said the judge. "I hereby sentence the defendant to a term of ten years in the Nevada State Prison. You will be eligible for parole in two years contingent upon good behavior."

I went numb, confused and scared. *What happened?* As court officers made their way toward me, pulling out handcuffs, I knew it had all gone horribly wrong. I turned to my dad. "What happened?"

"You're going to fuckin' prison, that's what happened."

CHAPTER 4

Who Runs This Place?

After my arrival at the Nevada State Prison, I stayed holed up in that roach-infested Fish Tank cell for about a week. My tears had dried, although I could still barely eat. Once my intake processing was complete, I was cleared for the general population in the "cellhouse," the prison's main facility, which housed roughly six hundred prisoners.

I turned in my oranges for prison-issued jeans, a navy T-shirt, and a pair of socks and sneakers. A guard led me through a maze of dingy halls till we reached my tier, a long row of barred gates—just like in the movies. Except this was no movie. The tier was dimly lit, and the smell was dank. I could feel the ugliness of the place. As we walked past the cells, convicts were inside, watching me through the bars. They all looked big, muscle-bound, tattooed—scary. I wanted to turn around and run—run as fast as I could.

When the guard pointed to an empty cell, I stepped in, relieved to at least escape the probing eyes. Without a word, he slammed the gate shut, locked it up, and walked away. I curled my fingers around the cold bars, watching as he disappeared from sight. *Two years . . . the judge said I'd be released in two years for good behavior. I can do this. Two years . . .*

In the days that followed, I became acquainted with the prison, however reluctantly. I paid close attention to the orders that were barked out on loudspeakers each day, announcing the prison basics—chow times, shower schedules, and lineups for daily rec. I did not want to make a mistake. When my tier was called for chow, I stepped out and stood on a silent line, waiting for the gate at the end of the tier to be unlocked.

Meals were dished out at the "culinary"—a fancy name for a chow hall fitted with round stainless-steel tables, where scary-looking men took their meals. The first thing that jumped out at me was that the tables were conspicuously divided by race. Blacks sat with Blacks, whites with whites, Native Americans sat with each other, and so on.

For my first meal, I stood holding my tray, unsure where to sit. A big white guy with a wide gap for front teeth motioned me to his table, where I grabbed a seat with him and two others. As I was seated, none of them looked at me, much less said anything. They barely talked among themselves for that matter. The whole place was quiet and tense. There wasn't a smile to be seen or a chuckle to be heard, the only sound being the scrape of cutlery against steel trays. With an allotted fifteen minutes to eat before the next tier filed in, I kept my eyes lowered and choked back a soggy hot dog, yearning for my mom's *spinenni*. Yearning for home.

The Nevada State Prison didn't offer any programs, activities, or structure to engage or improve one's situation. The center of daily life was the "yard." Each day, a guard shouted, "Yard turnout!" which was the signal for the tiers to file toward a narrow steel gate that led outside. In the minutes it took for it to be unlocked, the gate piled up with hundreds of cursing, edgy convicts who couldn't wait to turn loose. No sooner had the guards unlocked the gate, than they quickly disappeared as the men jostled and pushed through the narrow opening and out into the day.

The yard was nothing more than a dirt enclosure that sloped down from the cellhouse—a dismal scene of sand-colored dirt, broken rocks, and a chain-link fence enclosing a rundown basketball court. Not a tree, not a shrub, not a speck of greenery in sight.

The racial divides I had noted in the culinary were on prominent display in the yard. A large gathering of heavily tattooed white guys, about a hundred of them, banded together, while an equally formidable crew of Black convicts stood on the opposite side. Then there were the Mexicans in their own corner, wearing colorful beads around their necks, and in another huddle were the Native Americans, easily identifiable by their waist-length, jet-black hair.

These ethnic separations were surprising to me. On the outside, I was aware of racial tensions, of course, but it was nothing like this. I'd always been a "live and let live" kind of guy, so it was all a bit puzzling, but then again, I wasn't about to ask any questions.

In those early days, I just walked the yard's perimeter, my head down, hands in my pockets, feeling alone and conspicuous. Thankfully, no one seemed to notice me. They seemed to be in their own worlds, milling about, shooting hoops, doing chin-ups, pumping iron. Boom boxes blasted from every corner of the enclosure. I noticed that the tan-uniformed guards, walking in pairs, tended to skirt the edges of the yard. Up in the gun towers, guards holding high-powered rifles looked down on the scene.

The atmosphere in the yard felt the same as in the culinary—tense, like a fight could jump off at any moment. During my first week, it did. Some guy shouted at another that his music was too loud. His words were met with an angry shove, and hundreds rushed in for the slugfest. I looked up at the gun towers where the guards simply watched. On the ground, their tan-shirted counterparts scurried off in the opposite direction. A couple of cons finally got in and broke it up. But it wasn't over, not by a long shot. Later on, when yard was recalled and we were headed back into the cellhouse, a stream of blood spilled across the hall. Nobody said a word. Everybody just walked through it. I looked straight ahead and did the same.

Back at my cell, I wondered what had happened, hoping no one had been seriously hurt, although the amount of blood indicated otherwise. The following morning, I sat down for breakfast at what was becoming my regular table and listened for any talk of the fight, but there was none. It was the usual silence, and I dared not ask. I would never know what happened. I quietly ate my food. But I paid close attention to the grunts and little bits of conversation around the table. When any of them talked at all, it was about the favored topic—other people's charges.

At lunch one day, the gap-toothed guy motioned toward an older convict at a table across the room and whispered that his name was Greg Larson and that he was a "verified" stone-cold killer. The others nodded in admiration. Considering the relatively milder crime I'd committed, I wondered what they might think of me.

Apparently, people were starting to wonder about me, being a newcomer and probably the youngest one in the place. Passing by the big gang of white guys in the yard one morning, I felt someone's eyes boring into me, and I looked up. His entire face was lost in a jungle of tattooed snakes, and I couldn't even make out his eyes. I shuddered and moved along more quickly.

Several times a day, the crackling PA system blared out that the count was starting. This meant everyone had to leave the yard and return to their cells to be counted—a central feature of prison life—to be sure no one had escaped. As I headed in for the count one morning, a stooped old man that everybody called Pops stopped me and asked me what I was in for. For an instant, I was heartened. With a name like Pops, I thought he might be a friendly sort, someone to take me under his wing a little. But his cool blue eyes never warmed. I told him about my dog and the pickup truck and what I'd done in that crazy moment. He just grunted and turned to walk away. But before he did, I took a chance and asked him, "Hey, do you have any advice for me?"

He glared at me a long moment and hissed, "Expect the unexpected." Then he gimped away, leaving me to ponder his ominous message.

After a couple of weeks, others were also getting curious about me and began asking me about my charges. It seemed the nature of one's crime was critical information here. After I told them, I got a little bolder, asking them about their own offenses. The answers varied little—murder, attempted murder, armed robbery, and every other imaginable violent offense. *What was I doing in here?* Yeah, I'd driven a truck into a house. I guess I had some anger issues. But I was no killer, no robber, no ruthless drug dealer. Yet I was surrounded by them, and somehow, I had to navigate my way out.

At night I paced my cell, smoking cigarettes one after the next, my mind racing. I wanted no part of this place. I just wanted to do my two years and get the hell out. But I was starting to fear this was no simple matter. When I'd asked these guys about their own charges, I learned something that put the fear of God in me. Some of them said their initial crimes weren't all that different from mine—"nickel and dime stuff," as they referred to it. But the murder charges that had them locked up in here for decades, and even for life, happened right inside these prison walls, the result of deadly fights.

I was stunned. I thought you did your time and went home. I didn't even know that could happen. But I could not let it happen to me. I had no intention of being drawn into one of the bloody battles out in the yard that happened with regularity. But I also knew that at some point, I might need to fight.

During mealtimes, I had become aware of a table where the most forlorn convicts sat. It was called the knack table, and it was set aside for the "knacks," those who couldn't or wouldn't fight. The price they paid was constant exploitation—of their commissary, their integrity, their bodies. These were the utterly defeated souls of the prison, and I heard whispers that some of them simply ended their lives. There was no way in hell that I would ever take a seat at the knack table. I wasn't looking for trouble, but if it came my way, I would defend myself. But of course, I needed a spotless record when I went before the parole board in two years. I lit up another cigarette and kept pacing.

Back out in the yard, I continued to keep to myself, just observing, becoming more aware and seeking every edge I could find to better understand this place. Things were becoming more clearly defined. The white cons in the scary tattoos had a name – the Aryan Warriors. I gave them a wide berth, avoiding them as much as possible. The equally foreboding gang of Black convicts was the Black Mafia Family. The Native Americans were, unsurprisingly, the "Tribe." The Mexicans called themselves the MRUs for *Mi Raza Unida* ("My Race United"). Little offshoots of lesser gangs also stood huddled together.

Gang life loomed large in here; just how large was yet to be discovered. But my father's refrain—"Gangs are for cowards, don't ever join one"—had become *my* refrain. I wanted no part of them. Just as I had avoided outside street gangs, I fully intended to steer clear of them in here.

During the daytime, whether in the culinary or out in the yard, I was always on high alert. I had seen how the tiniest thing could set off a vicious fight. Within just a few weeks here, I had stepped over more than one pool of blood, and I'd gotten the uneasy feeling that concealed underneath every con's T-shirt was a sharp knife. It would be so easy to accidentally bump into someone or step on a sneaker, especially coming in and out of the yard where bottlenecks formed. There was no room for simple misunderstandings or quick apologies. I kept quiet and moved about ever so carefully. But when the day was done and we were locked in for the night, I exhaled a little. I figured the locked cells afforded a little more security. I figured wrong.

One night, after the lights had long been dimmed, and the tier had grown quiet, I had fallen into a restless sleep when I heard the rustle of footsteps. I hopped out of my bunk and over to the bars, where I caught sight of a lone figure racing down the tier. He was being chased by three others that I recognized as Aryan Warriors. I lost sight of them when they disappeared behind a column. But frantic shrieks followed: "No, no! Don't! Don't! Nooo!"

I retreated to my bunk and pulled my blanket about me, my heart pounding as the cries kept coming. With each shriek, I knew he was being stabbed. Just then, a guard came along, headed straight toward them, seemingly unaware of what he was walking into. *Hurry!*

The guard disappeared behind the column and, just as quickly, backpedaled out, muttering, "Oh, excuse me—excuse me." Then he turned and ran off.

Excuse me? Excuse me? What?!

Why hadn't he done something—blown a whistle, radioed for backup? *Anything?* So, the gangs could stab you, and the guards would run the other way? As I struggled to make sense of it, one question led to another. How had these Aryan Warriors even gotten out of their cells? We were all supposed to be locked in for the night. The only ones with the keys were the guards. My mind kept racing, trying to piece together what I'd just witnessed, but I kept coming back to the same frightening question: *Who runs this place?*

CHAPTER 5

In for a Penny

If inmates had a penny for every meaningful
rehabilitative program available to them,
they still couldn't afford a free cup of coffee.
—Post on Platform X: @Secrets from a Prison Cell

The first few months of my incarceration brought visits from home. But before anyone arrived, I had decided that family visits were not a good idea. As the reality of my situation was sinking in, I was doing a lot of hard thinking. While I had assumed that prison would be a harsh, scary existence, I did not expect this level of violence. Around every turn was a bloody fight, and I had already witnessed several men being stabbed.

But what especially disturbed me was the attitude of the guards. Instead of stepping in to stop fights, they seemed indifferent to them. The guards in the gun towers simply watched, while the ones on the ground ran in the opposite direction—or even became apologetic when they walked in on a stabbing. I had been raised to respect the badge, but what I saw in here was a far cry from what I would have expected. It was if there was a dark force operating in this prison, and the guards just wanted to skirt it, collect their paycheck, and go home—or they were in on it. If I got into some type of trouble, I didn't see how I could go to them for help. I couldn't trust them.

No, it was all on me. My prison existence would be no simple matter of minding my business and doing my time. If I was to make it out in two years, I could not lose my focus—not for one second. I couldn't have one foot in here and one foot out. I would see my family again once this was all over with.

When my mom arrived at the visit house, the sight of her about tore my heart out. With her pretty dress and sunny smile, she looked so out of place in this dungeon. She reached up to hug me. "Frankie!"

I hugged her tight and looked up at the ceiling, my lower lip quivering. *Take me home with you, Mom. Let's get out of here. Come on, let's go home.* I told her I was fine, and she seemed to believe it.

"Frankie," she asked, "Will they have a Christmas party at the holidays?" She was also very naive.

"No, Mom, there won't be any Christmas party."

We chatted about the recent heat wave and the latest doings with the neighbors. She brought me up to date on my sister, who was now a mother. Marie had gotten married a couple of years before I was arrested, and my mom showed me pictures of the grandkids.

As we neared our goodbyes, I needed to tell her about the decision I had made and how it would help me get out in two years' time. "Mom, I think it would be best that you don't come back."

"But Frankie . . ." she said, her eyes desperate and confused.

"It's just too painful, Mom. I promise that not having reminders of home right now is going to help me get through this. Let's write to each other, okay?"

"Oh, Frankie . . ."

I hugged her and urged her, "Now get going—you have a long drive back to Vegas."

She turned around before leaving. "I love you, Frankie," she said and blew me a kiss.

I would never see my mother again.

The next goodbye was Vivien. She flew into my arms, and my heart shattered into a thousand pieces. My Vivien. I held her close, wishing I could erase this nightmare and get back to our happy life together. How I wished we had celebrated her special eighteenth birthday the way we had planned it. I would at least have had that memory close to me while I got through this.

Then I steeled myself and took her by the shoulders. "We can't see each other anymore," I told her, letting my eyes sink into hers. "At least for the time being."

She looked at me with hurt and confusion. I knew it would be impossible for her to understand—for anyone on the outside to understand—what was necessary to survive life inside this prison. I tried to explain, telling her, "I can't be in here trying to hold us together and manage this place at the same time. It's better this way."

She cried, which made it so much harder.

"Two years is a long time, and hopefully we'll get back together when I get out. But don't wait for me. Get on with your life, Vivien."

After she was gone, it was a depressing walk back to my cell.

The visit with my dad wasn't as bad as saying goodbye to the women in my life. When he asked how I was doing, I was able to give him an honest account. He grunted and told me to hold my own, that sort of thing. He also agreed that it was best to shield my mother and sister from the reality of my prison life. Then he asked me what I wanted to do with my Impala. I told him to give it to Marie.

Although I was doing what I needed to do to survive, with each farewell to those I loved, the hardness I'd found so striking in the other prisoners was forming in me. Although I didn't realize it, the earliest erosion of my own humanity had begun.

I continued my vigilance and stayed to myself, especially in the crowded yard, which always felt dark, foreboding, and intense, even on the brightest of days. As I walked past the huddles of gangs, its members deep in conversation, the yard struck me as the stock exchange of the prison, the place where business was handled. I observed nods between prisoners and certain guards. Though cash was contraband, I saw plenty of green wads and small packages exchanging hands. I looked the other way. *See nothing, say nothing.*

I kept to the outskirts, sometimes stopping to watch a couple of guys sparring in a makeshift boxing ring, supposedly following more formal rules of boxing. But whether in the ring or in the middle of the yard, everything deteriorated into pretty much a dogfight anyway, which always attracted a crowd.

One afternoon, a guy nicknamed "Thumper" and Greg Larson, the "verified" stone-cold killer, came to blows, and I had a front-row seat to the match. Larson was referred to as the white version of Muhammad Ali. Thumper was a biker, six-foot-eight and tough. Larson, though muscular and strong, was only five-foot-seven or -eight, but what he lacked in size he more than made up for in power. Nobody was going to miss this one. The guards in the tower leaned against the railings to watch, while their peers on the ground abandoned their posts and hustled out to join the convicts on the sidelines. The fight lasted all of ten minutes and consisted of nothing but hard clean punches thrown by both men, without any wrestling involved. When both cons were spent, Thumper said, "It's done." Then the two of them went to the hospital.

Larson and Thumper were intriguing to me, and not only because of their fighting prowess. They were both highly regarded by the other convicts, yet neither of them belonged to a gang. They were known as "Independents." The fact that nobody would dream of messing with either one of them gave me hope and signaled that being an Independent could be my pathway out of here. They blazed their own trail, and that's exactly what I intended to do.

But if no one would mess with them, I was as of yet untested, which wasn't going to last much longer. I was beginning to get sideways glances, like I was being sized up for bullying, commissary money—and God knows what else. I knew I could fight, and I just wanted to get it over with and establish myself as someone to be left alone. I knew that was the only way to garner some semblance of respect.

And then it came. I was standing on the culinary line when somebody shoved me, and I knew it was deliberate. Reflexively, I slugged him. He went down fast. The culinary got real quiet. Though I was quivering inside, I calmly assumed my place back in the line. I wanted every con in that chow hall to see that nineteen-year-old Frank De Palma could hold his own, that I wasn't someone to be messed with.

A few weeks later, a similar provocation occurred, and once again I prevailed. I held my head a little higher after that, and even detected nods from a few grizzled faces. I'd earned some respect—exactly what I needed. I was never so grateful for my street-fighting skills.

But just as I was starting to feel confident, I got my ass handed to me. It started out in a silly argument with somebody a few cells down from me. The voice was unfamiliar. But the war of words heated up. "I'll see you outside," he challenged. I knew I couldn't back down, so when the cell doors unlocked, I bolted out, ready to go. And there he stood, arms crossed, grinning at me. It was none other than Thumper, the behemoth biker. *Oh shit!* But there was no way out of this. Every con on that tier was watching.

Like a crazy man, I charged him and landed the first punch, leveling him. He seemed a little surprised, but he was right back on his feet, and this time I went down—again, and again, and again. The guy was so big, it was like fighting a goddamned grizzly bear. The third time I hit the ground, I was done. He let out a belly laugh and reached out a hand to pull me up, saying, "You got good hands." Coming from him, I kind of appreciated that. I got whooped, all right, but I took consolation knowing that at least I'd made it clear I wasn't afraid to fight—and to fight someone of Thumper's size and strength. There had been a little victory, after all.

At the infirmary, I learned the full extent of the damage—a couple of busted ribs, a broken nose, and a hairline jaw fracture. As I gimped back to my cell, I figured it was a small price to pay for the statement I had made. Hopefully, I would now be left alone for good.

Fighting was the mainstay of prison entertainment, borne largely out of boredom. Devoid of normal activities like going to work, raising a family, and planning for a future, prison life was an unnatural existence. It was a life frozen in nothingness, of deadly monotony, one endlessly boring day after the next. But things at the Nevada State Prison did liven up a little on the weekends. Surprisingly, the prison operated a casino. When Friday night rolled around, the fourth floor of the cellhouse came to life with the scent of exotic-smelling tobacco drifting down to the tiers. Come the weekend, convicts with a little money could gamble, drink, and have a fine time right inside the prison walls. I guess it was only fitting that in the state known for gaming, the gambling life should extend into its prison.

The casino had actually been operating for decades, beginning in the 1930s. At one time, it even had its own separate building, right on the prison grounds. But in 1967, a warden named Carl Hocker shut it down—at least officially.

The Hocker era was just before my time, but the story of how the casino was quietly resurrected was the subject of oft-repeated lore about the Aryan Warriors and Hocker himself. Apparently, the Warriors had been heavily involved in the casino and its profits, often resulting in violent encounters between Aryan Warriors and prison officials not only inside prison walls but also on the outside, where released Warriors took orders from their imprisoned shot caller, a guy named Pat McKenna. Inside the prison, McKenna's name was uttered in fearful whispers. Out in the yard, whenever I dared a glance at the Warrior huddle, it was McKenna who stood at their center. He appeared about ten years older than I was, and it was with the aura of a sinister general that he commanded his vicious troops.

The story had it that a deal to reopen a more modest casino was hashed out between Hocker and McKenna in a midnight meeting in the yard. In exchange for the reinstitution of the casino, Hocker reportedly said, "My officers go home safe at night. My officers are not to be touched."

Now, I don't know if this is exactly what was said or if this fabled meeting even took place. But what I can say is that when I arrived at the Nevada State Prison, the casino was in full swing. What I can also say is that such an agreement would help explain the power of the Aryan Warriors inside the prison.

As enticing as the casino sounded, I had no interest in any of it. Even if I had money, which I did not, the casino was a deeper immersion into the prison culture, and I did not care to move in that direction. My sole interest was to get out.

But a two-year release would take more than vigilance. My mind kept flitting back to my fight with Thumper. It bothered me how easily I'd been beaten by him and how winded I'd been afterward. I needed to up my game. I put down the cigarettes I smoked each day—cold turkey. And though I was constantly shadowboxing in my cell, honing my moves, it wasn't enough. I needed to get stronger. I focused on the weight bench out in the yard. I'd never lifted weights before, but one afternoon, I stood at the end of the line. When it was my turn, I lay down on the bench, looked up at the wide Nevada sky, clenched the barbell, and lifted.

CHAPTER 6

A Rejected Offer

From the beginning, I yearned for a friend—someone to talk to, to joke around with, to count the days till we both went home. But friendship was a liability in prison. Friendship requires trust, and there was no trust, only suspicion, hatred, and murderous intent.

The criminals surrounding me were one-dimensional. It seemed like all the good stuff on the human spectrum of emotions—warmth, good will, humor, compassion—had been lopped off, leaving only the shadow side intact and intensified. Many were doomed to this place for the rest of their lives. I guess the years of confinement with no hope for anything other than this depressing existence could do that to a person.

The gangs offered some sort of kinship, but it was all superficial. They would turn on each other in a deadly fashion, as I had learned in the aftermath of that late-night tier attack by the Aryan Warriors. Though everything was hush-hush in the days that followed, through the whispers, I eventually found out that the guy survived it. I also learned that he was an Aryan Warrior himself. The attack was because he was suspected of snitching—of being a "rat"—so his "brothers" turned on him. No one was ever held accountable. But everyone knew it had been ordered by Warrior leader, Pat McKenna.

As the months crawled along, my routine consisted of leaving my cell, walking laps in the yard, and lifting weights. In the evenings, I would sit on my bunk and listen to music and late-night talk shows on the radio that my father had mailed me. My favorite was Art Bell's show *Coast to Coast*. I looked forward to his program during the day and listened to it every night. The radio kept me company in my otherwise lonely and fearful existence.

But in the absence of friendship, there was respect. One convict who had made an impression on me was a Black guy named Cal Wilson. We only knew each other a couple of months before he disappeared. People came and went from the prison, and you never knew why. I met Cal at the weight bench where he offered me badly needed pointers on form and technique. Cal was ripped, very defined, very impressive. I saw Cal take on four guards at once, and he wiped the floor with them. He didn't cause problems, but if they came his way, he wasn't afraid to finish them. Cal was highly respected by others. Like me, he was an Independent. He had no interest in the Black Mafia Family (or BMF as they were called), just as I had no interest in gang life. Even so, we were well aware that the prison's powerful racial divides could pit us against each other if it came down to it. It had been made clear to both of us that, Independent or not, if gang warfare broke out, we were to side with our respective races. Failure to do so was worse than being a snitch; it meant automatic death.

Occasionally, there was also cause for gang unity. If prison officials began infringing upon established prisoner boundaries, then racial issues were put on the back burner, and everyone—the Aryan Warriors, the Tribe, the BMF, Mi Raza Unida, and the Independents—all came together as one against the prisoners' mutual nemesis—the man, the guards, the administration. And this coming together is exactly what happened in a dispute with the prison administration over our food.

The meals that were glopped out onto the metal trays were god-awful. But when a mystery meat was introduced into the menu, it was not only regarded with suspicion but nausea, smelling like dog shit. It was served a few times, and whatever it was, it was truly revolting. This called for a meeting of the gang heads. Together, they complained to prison officials. It was agreed that this item would be removed from the menu. But when it got served again, every able-bodied man was called to action, resulting in a full-blown riot in the culinary. In a fury that energized all-out destruction, Cal and I dutifully joined in. We trashed tables, knocked down plexiglass barriers, smashed light fixtures and heating elements, and destroyed anything else we could get our hands on.

When the riot ended, the kitchen was in ruins, and the entire prison was placed on lockdown. For three months, we were confined to our cells and ate nothing but baloney sandwiches for breakfast, lunch, and dinner. It would be months before the culinary was restored. But that horrible meat was never served again.

The reopening of the culinary marked one year that I'd been at the Nevada State Prison. It had been a tough, scary existence, but I'd managed to hold my own, all the while clinging to my hopes for a favorable impression with the parole board, now one year away. Twelve more months and this place would be a bad memory. I counted every day down, from the hours to the minutes. *Six hours till midnight—one more day down. Three more days till the end of the week. One week left in the month, eleven months to go.* Each day down brought me closer to my family, to Vivien, and to the canyons and streams where Bud and I had gone camping.

Over that first year, my family had respected my wishes and refrained from visiting. I spoke with my dad on the phone from time to time and kept him up to date. Because my mom was deaf, phone calls weren't possible, but she sent me little cards with X's and O's that lifted my spirits. As for Vivien, I banished her from my thoughts. At one point, I received a thick envelope from her containing what must have been a long letter. I held it in my hands, agonizing about opening it, fearful it would stir up strong emotions that could throw me off my game. For days I looked at the envelope, held it in my hands, pressed it to my heart. In the end, I decided I couldn't afford to take the chance of learning that she was still waiting for me, or worse, that she'd moved on and never wanted to see me again. Maybe someday I could explain it all to her. I gritted my teeth and threw out the unopened envelope and headed to the yard to work out.

Although I fought to stay on the fringes of prison life, over the course of the year, I was inevitably absorbing the unspoken codes that were essential to survival. The cardinal rules were mind your business, don't ask questions, and above all else, never snitch—never report anything to prison officials, ever.

There was disgust not only for rats, but for rapists and child molesters. Most sexual offenders were housed at the Northern Nevada Correctional Center a few miles down the road from the Nevada State Prison—but not everyone. Those rapists who made it into the prison didn't last long. One time, a couple of guards were walking a sex offender through the yard. They made it halfway across before a band of Aryan Warriors waving shovels descended, howling, "Rapo!" The guards bolted, and the Warriors knocked the guy to the ground and bashed his head with the shovels. Pat McKenna looked on, nodding his approval. The guy survived it but suffered permanent brain damage.

As for me, I got into a few more fistfights, but thankfully, nothing rose to the level of tarnishing my crucial conduct record. After a while, the scuffles dropped off, and I was left alone. I had achieved my goal. I had established myself as a capable fighter, and it had been noted. But little did I know that it had been noted in ways I never could have foreseen. My carefully calculated efforts had actually paved the way to catastrophe.

The first inkling of trouble came when an Aryan soldier

showed up at my cell to deliver a message. He said Pat McKenna wished to have a word with me in the yard. I was immediately alarmed. What would the head of the Aryan Warriors want with me? I had never had a personal encounter or direct contact with him. I would have liked to have sent a return message: *No thanks!* But I couldn't. McKenna was far too dangerous to dismiss.

At the appointed time, I walked out to the yard, hoping the meeting would be quick. There he was, standing alone, waiting for me. As I got closer, I was surprised by McKenna's clean-cut appearance. Unlike the scary-looking horde he ruled over, his curly hair was short, neatly kempt, and his face and neck were devoid of tattoos. He had straight white teeth. Were it not for his cold eyes, he could have been the boy next door.

"Do you know who I am?" he asked.

I nodded.

"What do you think of my organization?"

I shrugged and mumbled something polite.

"Well, I've been observing you since you got here. I have others watching you, too. And from all observations and reports," he said, "I like the way you handle yourself."

My stomach twisted.

"I think you would be an asset to my organization. In fact, I want to personally take you under my wing and teach you in the ways of a real man, in the ways of the Warrior."

For a moment, it was all surreal. It didn't seem possible. Here I was, standing in the recreation yard of the Nevada State Prison, face to face with the shot caller of the Aryan Warriors, a gang I'd never even heard of a year earlier. But I didn't have to think about my answer. There was no way. I had no interest in white supremacy, in gangs, in any of it.

"Thank you," I said, carefully. "I'm just not interested in gang life. It's something my father instilled in me when I was a kid. My father taught me how to be a man, at least up to now, and I hope life will teach me the rest." I assured him, though, that if it came down to a race riot, I'd be where I needed to be, hoping that might satisfy him. "I just wanted to finish out my time and go home," I added, naive to think he'd give a shit.

He looked startled. "You're saying no to me?"

"Yes, I am."

His eyes narrowed, and he stared at me for a moment. Then he flicked his fingers across his shoulder as if he was whisking away debris, making a point to stomp on it as it hit the ground. Then he glared at me. "You're dismissed."

The walk back across the yard seemed to take forever, my legs wobbling the whole way. When I got back to my cell, I sat on my bunk, playing the meeting over and over in my head, wishing it hadn't happened and that I'd imagined it. But it was real, and I was scared. Had I just made a big mistake? *No!* I couldn't possibly become an Aryan Warrior. *My God!* I told myself I had every right to say no, every right to continue as an Independent. I told myself it would blow over and that it would all be fine. I didn't sleep the entire night.

Back out in the yard the next day, everything seemed the same. No one said anything to me or gave me any reason to believe I had a problem. The Warriors were huddled around their leader, who never gave me another look.

To ease my nerves, out of sheer desperation, I sought out Greg Larson, the stone-cold killer. I was particularly interested in him because he was an Independent, and I wanted to know if he'd ever turned down a Warrior invitation. Larson had a deep voice, intense dark eyes, and a powerful presence. Aside from his fighting prowess, he had also stabbed a couple of prisoners who had nearly died. I didn't need anyone to tell me that he was an extremely dangerous man. I felt it. But at that point, I didn't care.

As I laid it out for him, his eyes widened, and he interrupted me before I'd even finished. "You got a problem, youngster."

He confirmed that he'd been asked to join the gang and declined, without issue. "But here's the difference," he said. "I wasn't invited by McKenna himself. You rejected the shot caller's personal invitation. He'll take that as a slap in the face, and he won't forget. He's a dangerous guy. He controls the other gang heads, the guards, and pretty much the whole prison. He sees himself as some kind of warrior and sage all rolled into one, and anyone who doesn't kowtow to his ego better be looking over his shoulder. He's also a cool manipulator—he likes to play with people before he goes in for the kill, so watch your back."

This was a disaster.

If Greg Larson's take on the matter hadn't underscored the danger I now faced, a late-night incident a couple of days later surely did. I was half asleep when, once again, I was awakened by footsteps on the tier. But this time, there was no running. The footsteps were deliberate, and they came to a stop outside a cell just down from me. I crept out of my bunk and peered through the bars. I knew the guy in that cell. His name was Sammy Medina. I could just make out the face of one of the guards, along with three Warriors. The guard unlocked Sammy's gate and stood back while the cons rushed in. I strained to hear what sounded like muffled commotion. Some minutes later, the three of them emerged, and the guard locked the gate. Everything fell quiet again.

Early the next morning, I was awakened by shouts. I jumped up and gripped the bars to see what was going on. Outside Sammy's cell, I recognized the same guard from the night before, yelling into his radio, "We got a hanger! Man hanging!"

I sunk back on my cot, dazed. They killed him. They killed Sammy. Those three Aryan Warriors hanged him. The guard announcing the "suicide" must have been on their payroll. *Oh my God!*

The murder was surely on orders from their ruthless leader, the very person I had just insulted. Sammy Medina wasn't a bad guy. *Oh, Jesus!* What did this mean for me? Could I now expect a late-night visit like this? Would it be my payback for rejecting McKenna's offer? Would he go that far? I just didn't know. I broke into a cold sweat, praying to God, "Please show me some way out of this nightmare."

CHAPTER 7

Expect the Unexpected

After Sammy Medina's murder, I was crazed. I paced my cell like the caged animal I was. Prior to the McKenna yard encounter, I'd thought I had a decent chance of getting out of here. But now my focus shifted from the countdown calendar to staying alive. I barely slept, and when yard was called, I raced out to the weight bench. I had started out pressing 125 pounds; now I was moving in on 200. My hair had been on the longish side, and I feared it could be grabbed too easily in a fight, so I had an inmate barber cut it short. In the corner of my cell was a long-handled wooden scrub brush that I used to clean my toilet. I decided it would make a nice solid club. I placed it close to the head of my bunk, hidden from view but within easy reach should I need it. The words of advice that old Pops had initially given me reverberated: *Expect the unexpected.*

As I lay on my bunk in the evenings, everything felt bleak and dark. I kept looking around my cell, double-checking that my scrub brush was secure. I could not control what might come my way. But if McKenna was coming for me, of one thing I was certain: I would not go down without a fight.

I think it was a weeknight. I'd gotten up to wash my hands when four Black cons strolled into my cell without asking permission. I dried my hands fast. This was not the way things were done in here. Respect was paramount, and not to be respectful of one's space could cause things to get crazy real fast. They were all smiles, but I immediately sensed something was up. As the cells were narrow in width, all four were somewhat bunched up and they had to spread out a little. I had been standing by the sink and was within easy reach of my hardwood brush. Fear flooded into me the same way it had when I was out in the streets and about to have a fight. Along with it came a rush of adrenalized energy. I was ready for anything, even though being ready meant little when it was one against four, none of whom were small by any means.

I recognized two of them as members of the BMF. One was known as Copper Slim, and by noticing the reverence others showed him in the yard, I knew he held a high position in their ranks. The second one was Knuckles, a rather ugly guy. He was one of their enforcers. The other two were just a couple of gophers.

Copper began making small talk as his eyes were roving over my belongings. I sensed he was scanning for anything I could use as a weapon. He looked me over. "So how you doing, man? I notice you stay to yourself. What are you in for, anyway? How much time you got?"

I did my best to look calm and responded to his questions as casually as I could.

"So, have you chosen yet?" he asked.

I was confused as I thought he was asking me if I had chosen what gang I would run with. It was a stupid question as no one would run with anyone outside their race. "I don't run with any-body—I'm an Independent. Your question doesn't make sense."

Copper laughed and said, "No, no, baby. What I mean is, a pretty young thing like you needs someone to take care of you."

I saw Knuckles tense up, and I knew what was up. Fear, anger, disgust, and panic flooded my veins, and I grabbed the hardwood handle and swung it at Knuckles, who was the big-ger of the two. I clocked him in the cheek. He dropped down, holding his face. The two gophers took off.

Copper Slim punched me in the forehead. He stumbled, and I hit him hard and solid in the head above his right ear. I swung and hit him again in the head, and then I began swinging fast and hard at both Copper and Knuckles, connecting easily. Knuckles bolted from the cell, stumbling out into the tier bars.

Copper was on his knees covering his head with his arms. I stopped when I saw how badly his head was bleeding. Blood was on the wall, on his hands and arms and clothes. As he moaned, I got scared and backed away. Two Aryan Warriors ran in to see what was going on. I shouted, "They were trying to fuckin' rape me!"

They told me to clean up, give the club to the guy on my right, and to stay in the cell. The two of them helped Copper Slim down the tier to a couple of his people. Knuckles had gotten a knife and told the Aryans that it was just him and me now, but I heard the Warriors tell him they brought the BS to me and got their asses handed to them. They said there would be no more bloodshed that night, and that if I was moved on, then there would be a whole lot more blood spilling.

One of the Warriors came back to my cell and said, "Copper Slim is their number two, so you got problems, youngster. We can't do any more for you than we just did. You're on your own." Before he left, he added, "You're all right with me."

I slid my gate shut and finished cleaning up and changed my pants. I knocked on the cell wall to my right. An old man reached his arm out through the bars, and I passed my hardwood brush to him. That was that. The guards were summoned on a "man down" call. The entire tier was placed on lockdown until later that night when the shift lieutenant and the cellhouse sergeant came up and pulled out one of the Aryans and one of the BMF, and they all left. Within the hour, they returned, and the guards spoke loudly for all to hear. They told us that the personal issues had been resolved and everyone was friends again and that everything would go back to usual come dawn. They left.

Afterward, it was very quiet except for the intermittent flushing of a toilet or someone coughing. I didn't sleep that night, thinking about what had happened. Twenty-four hours earlier, I was minding my own business, bothering no one. Four guys had come into my cell and tried to rape me, and I had defended myself with everything I had. *What else was I supposed to do?*

At 5:30 a.m., the dead bolt locking the cell doors was disengaged. We could still open and close our sliding barred doors, but we couldn't lock them. It bothered me that I couldn't keep my cell gate locked. We wouldn't be released to chow until around 6:15 a.m. I stood in the doorway of my cell wishing I still had my wooden brush. I felt vulnerable without it. A few cons milled about, and one of the Aryans told me that Copper Slim was okay but he'd had to go to the hospital in town and that Knuckles was hurting pretty bad, too. He warned me not to get lax.

It seemed to take forever, but finally the guards released our tier for breakfast. On the mess hall line, a hard-looking white con walked toward me. I recognized him as a high-ranking shot caller for the Aryan Warriors. He motioned me toward his table. "Siddown, youngster."

I did as I was told. He said his name was "Old Folks." With his salt-and-pepper beard, he did seem old to me, but looking back, he was probably no more than thirty. But I was less interested in his moniker than in what he had to say.

"Listen, kid, you need to start watching your back at all times. You injured a high-ranking member of the BMF, and they've put out a green light on you. You know what that means?"

I shook my head no.

"Green-lighted means you're to be killed on sight. The BMF wants you dead."

He was quiet for a moment as I struggled to take it in.

"They will send their soldiers, their recruits, anyone they've got to kill you. And I've got more bad news. Pat McKenna has ordered that no one is to help you out—not the Aryan Warriors or the Independents or any of the other gangs. No one in this prison is to come to your defense. You'll be completely on your own fighting this gang. You've got two options—one, be a sheep and it's over with fast, or two, be a wolf and fight. I'm sorry to have to put it like this, but if you're going to die, then die like a man."

I had no words.

"Someone will visit you later," he added. "Pay attention."

I headed back for my cell in a trance, unable to comprehend any of this.

As promised, that evening, an Aryan soldier came to my cell and pulled two long pieces of steel from his pants. One was sharpened to a point; the other wasn't. Both weapons were about ten inches in length and just over an inch wide. "These are from a friend," he said. "Because of Pat McKenna's order, this is all anyone can do for you."

He then explained to me that blades were more effective than ice picks because the flats could be twisted, doing heavier damage. Before he left, he said, "From now on you have to make your own shanks, but no one will deny you a blank if you need one."

After he was gone, I sat still on my bunk, pinching myself to wake up from this nightmare. But it was useless. I was fully awake, and I had been "green-lighted"—targeted for murder by a gang of about eighty violent cons, each one looking to make a name for himself. There was no place to hide, and no one to come to my aide. How the hell would I survive? I likely wouldn't, and the best I could hope for . . . *was to die like a man?* My whole body shook.

How had it all happened? I'd never had any issues with the BMF before. Was McKenna behind it? Had he orchestrated this rape attempt to punish me? I kept hearing Greg Larson's words: "He controls the other gang heads . . . He likes to play with people before he goes in for the kill . . ."

Was this it? Had he set this up to degrade me and then watch me fight to stay alive afterwards? This guy was pure evil.

Regardless of what was behind it all, I had invoked the wrath of the BMF. I stared at the two cold lengths of steel that lay on my blanket.

Was I a sheep or a wolf?

CHAPTER 8

A Sitting Duck

You must have a plan if they come in with shanks. What will I use to block? Do I have something to stop the blood? . . . If not, you are a sitting duck waiting for death.
—Post on Platform X: @Secrets from a Prison Cell

It took over a week to do it, but late at night, on the floor at the back of my cell, I sharpened the blank sheets of steel until they had the look of bayonets, with sharp tips and edges. Though I had been in numerous fistfights, I had never been in a knife fight. Handling the shanks felt strange. I buried one of them inside my mattress along with a long strip of sheeting to be wrapped around it for a handle. The other knife I would keep with me at all times, even when I showered and went to the yard. I took Old Folks's chilling message to heart. Pat-down searches by the guards were rare so I wasn't worried about my knife being discovered. However, having a knife did little to alleviate my anxieties and fear. But at least I would not be completely defenseless.

At this point, I seriously considered going to prison officials and asking for help. But this was no simple decision; I played it over and over in my mind. I had personally witnessed their own criminality and corruption. I could not shake the image of the guard who had essentially apologized to the Aryan Warriors for walking in on them during a stabbing. And, of course, there was the Sammy Medina murder, facilitated by a guard. I was haunted by it. More recently, a guy suspected of being a snitch had been stabbed to death in the yard by the Warriors. As he lay bleeding on the ground, prison officials stood around, taking forever to summon medical help. There was no urgency. They did not care about him. Why would they care about me?

But it was more than that. I was beginning to hate them. The guards looked upon us as less than human, never calling us by our names but by our "back numbers," our official prison ID numbers. They told us to our faces that we were scumbags, idiots, and a waste of taxpayer money. I saw one con, fed up with the verbal abuse, lash out at a guard. The guard just nodded and smiled. Later that day, he came back with a couple of other guards, and they walked the angry con off the tier. An hour went by before he returned, appearing physically unscathed, but visibly shaken.

Since any private conversations with guards were eyed suspiciously and suggested the inmate might be an informant, he was panic-stricken. He insisted they'd just taken him to some empty room and had him sit there to create the impression that he was an informant—a snitch. Everyone was looking, watching, speculating, undecided whether or not to believe him. The horror of being stabbed was equal to the terror of looking over your shoulder in fear of it.

No one in prison was in deadlier danger than the despised snitch. For me to seek help from prison authorities would have put me squarely into the snitch category. If I went to them, they'd have unending questions—*Who said you'd been greenlighted? Who delivered shanks to your cell?* It would be one thing after the next, and I would have no way of knowing if the officials I was speaking to were on the Warrior payroll. Would I be setting myself up for a deadly, late-night cell visit? I couldn't risk it. I was on my own.

Two months passed after those four convicts made their ugly play for me. It had been two months of nothing more than hard stares from BMF members, and a few whispered threats. I kept to my program of staying to myself, and if I wasn't on the yard, I was in my cell. I was afraid, very much so, but fear was no stranger to me. I'd known fear my whole life. Fear kept me alert.

When those two months passed by without incident, I began to grasp at a little hope, wondering if perhaps I was respected for how I stood up for myself. I had earned the right to be left alone. Or perhaps Old Folks had quietly spoken to others on my behalf. He seemed to like me, calling me "youngster" and "son." I felt cautiously optimistic. After another couple of months passed by, I felt a growing sense of confidence that my issues had been laid to rest and that I could get on with the task of getting out of here. Eight months remained till I went before the parole board.

I removed the cloth handle from my knife but hid it in a spot that afforded me quick access to it. The other one was still inside my mattress. Another week of calm passed by when, early one morning, I woke up suddenly, thinking I had been called by name. It was very dark except for the yellow 40-watt light bulb on the tier that cast a sickly pale glow and served as a night light for the guards. It was eerily quiet. I hurriedly got dressed, listening carefully for what, I didn't know. But I listened.

Suddenly, I felt a strange, intense sensation within. It felt like some dial had been turned and caused the world to move in slow motion. The atmosphere felt heavy, the air dense. I felt very keen, alert, on edge, yet at the same time, I felt a strong sense of calm that held a kind of euphoria unlike that produced by any drug. I felt afraid, yet very much in control. I got my knife and soaked the long strip of sheet in the toilet. I carefully wrapped the blade with it, tying it tight. It wasn't coming off.

There were about six inches of sharpened steel showing. I placed it on my bed and covered it with my T-shirt. I sat there, afraid, yet quietly calm. A short time later, a guard walked by, saw me, and said, "5 a.m." That was the final count of the night. The next count would be at 11:30 a.m.

At 5:30, the guard came upstairs and disengaged the dead-bolt lock, which allowed us to slide our steel-barred doors open and shut at will. Generally, I was the first prisoner up and about, but that morning, as I stepped from my cell, I saw four convicts standing at the far end of the tier. I recognized one of them as one of the four who had come into my cell that night just over four months back. I knew at that moment that nothing was over, and though I was in trouble, I still had a feeling of quiet calm and energy flowing through me.

I eased back into the cell, picked up my knife, and saw my hand was shaking. I could feel my heart pounding in my chest. I stepped from the cell, knife held on my left thigh, and saw that the four cons were now just two cells away. Two of them had knives in their hands. What I did next surprised them as much as it did me. I rushed them, swinging my knife as my body slammed into them. I heard a hard grunt and felt my knife sink into the body of one of my attackers. It sounded like a shovel going into soft, wet sand. I just kept trying to go forward, slicing wildly at the air. I felt hard blows to my face and head, and I began having a difficult time pulling air into my lungs.

The thought of dying filled me with panic and desperation. I gave everything I had. I heard one of the four yell in pain as I felt my knife hit something. I didn't realize that two of my attackers were out of the fight. I felt an intensely sharp, wrenching pain in my knee, but for some reason, I didn't go down. I couldn't draw any air into my lungs. I felt arms pulling hard at me and saw more convicts, both Black and white, grabbing me, my knife still waving through the air. I was struggling against this new threat. I felt my knife being pulled from my hand and tried to yell, but no sound came out. I heard a voice telling me repeatedly, "It's over. It's over. Let it go."

I had no more fight in me; I couldn't breathe, my lungs were on fire, my head felt too heavy to hold up. There was so much blood all over me, as well as on the other cons holding me down.

I later found out that I had stabbed two of them. One had been hit in the chest, puncturing a lung, and he had also sustained lacerations to his face and arms. The other had a stab wound to his neck and two puncture wounds to his arm. I suffered a broken nose, a hairline jaw fracture, a broken cheekbone, one stab wound in my right side, and a deep stab wound just above my right knee with what someone later told me was a bone crusher. But I was alive. I laid there on the floor while someone yelled, "Man down on 2-B-East."

Before more guards arrived, one of the Warriors said to me, "Hold your mud, gunslinger, hold your mud." I didn't understand at the time that he meant for me to keep my mouth shut and don't tell.

Well, no one died, and everybody held their mud. After all the confusion and chaos of guards running around with walkie-talkies, yelling for ambulances, I found myself on the way to the hospital. A guard named Murphy accompanied me in the ambulance. "Hang in there, kid," he said. "This will all go away."

It would never go away. But then again, neither would the memory of this man's unusual kindness.

I was admitted into a hospital in Carson City, where I was x-rayed and poked by nurses and doctors, asked questions, and given a shot for the pain, which did wonders. The hospital was such a welcome relief from prison. I felt like a school kid, waiting for the nurses to smile and fuss over me awhile. I really just wanted to feel like a normal person.

Two days later, a prison guard, Lieutenant Michael Harrison, arrived at my bedside. A real hater, as his kind were referred to by the cons, he'd made it clear he despised us and went out of his way to withhold any form of human decency whenever he had the opportunity.

He sat down in a chair, spoke into some cassette recorder, stated who he was, why he was there, and who he was interviewing. "Now," he said to me. "I want you to state your name, back number, and answer my questions with honest and direct responses. Do you understand?"

I nodded that I did and told him my name and back number.

"Tell me exactly what happened."

I spoke without any thought to what I was going to say. It came out rather naturally. I told him I'd somehow gotten caught up in someone else's fight. "It happened so fast that I never saw anyone's face."

He asked if I was affiliated with any prison gang, especially the Aryan Warriors.

"No," I said. "I don't have any ties to any gang factions in the prison."

"Are you able to walk the line without problems?"

"Yes."

"Do you have any problems or fears with any inmates at the prison—or are you a target of any gang?"

"No," I said. I dared not tell him the truth. The Nevada State Prison was controlled by the gangs—not him.

After he was done with his questions, he handed me a form to sign. It was a liability release, which freed prison officials from responsibility should any harm befall me and stated that I was signing it voluntarily. I signed it. Then he stood up and looked down at me. He appeared to be about my father's age. I had just turned twenty-one, and for a split second, I foolishly hoped his face might soften toward me. But he just looked at me in an ugly sort of way. "I'll see you next time—if you live, that is."

Three days into my hospital stay, a nurse told me I was being released the following day. She said I would make a complete recovery, and though my knee would hurt for months to come and would still take a couple of months to walk on, ultimately, it would be fine.

When she left, the reality of my life filled me with such fears and uncertainties that I felt I would go insane. I thought about calling the nurse or a doctor and telling them what really happened, why it happened. I wanted them to know that I wasn't a bad person. I just wanted to be free of that prison. I had lots of wild, hope-filled thoughts and ideas. But as the doctors examined me for the last time, I said nothing.

The next afternoon, I was released from a real hospital in a real world where real people lived and was returned to another world that wasn't supposed to be but was surely, slowly becoming my world.

CHAPTER 9

Walking Through Hell

*If your path demands you walk through
hell, walk as if you own the place.*
—AUTHOR UNKNOWN

After my release from the hospital, I stayed in the prison infirmary for close to two months. I was still in a good deal of pain, but unlike the hospital, I received little medical attention to relieve it. But like everything else in that place, you just learned to deal with it and do your best.

A month after I'd returned to the prison, a sergeant brought me two write-ups. One was for fighting, for which I received five days in the hole, to be served at some later date to be determined.

The second offense was for possession of the hidden knife, which was found in my mattress when the guards rolled up my property after the fight. The penalty for this was pending decision by the suits in Carson City. There was a question as to whether criminal charges would be filed against me. The sergeant said he felt such a charge would be a waste of people's time and money and that most would just toss the blade, but unfortunately for me, Lieutenant Harrison, the "hater" who'd taken my statement at the hospital, ordered it to be bagged and written up. I had a very bad feeling.

A week later, my worst fear was realized: I had a new

charge—possession of a sharp instrument, namely, a homemade knife. Court proceedings were swift, and I received a sentence of three years.

With this additional case, my hopes of being released from prison in two years were gone. Lying in bed at night, I sobbed into my pillow. My imaginings of going home soon were nothing more than a cruel fantasy. I wasn't going anywhere. Again and again, I asked myself where I had gone wrong. By refusing McKenna's offer to join the Aryan Warriors? I thought I was doing the right thing by not joining a gang. But maybe I should have. If I had become a Warrior, none of this would have happened.

But, on the other hand, had I joined the vicious gang, I likely wouldn't have fared much better. Gang indoctrination comes at a price. I would have had to "make my bones," which meant to hurt or kill someone. As McKenna's protégé, I would have been at his beck and call, carrying out all kinds of violent assignments that would have just as quickly landed me in the same position I was in now. At least these charges came about in a more honorable way than some cheap gang move. At least that's what I told myself. I was grasping at anything I could to offset the anguish of not going home.

But I had little time for contemplation. I was in deadly danger. That I had not only survived the attack but injured my assailants in the process only upped the BMF's bounty on my head.

In a frantic phone call with my father, I told him what I expected to happen next. "I'm a dead man, Dad. I'll never get out of here alive. They'd already had a green light out on me—to kill me on sight. And now with this? It's just a matter of time."

"Now, listen, Frank. Can I call someone?"

I was surprised by my father's concerned tone. At a time when I felt so alone, I felt an unexpected rush of gratitude for this man—the only person in my corner.

"Listen," he said, "I'll call the warden—"

"No! No! Don't do that. Please! You have no idea what it's like in here. The guards are worse than the prisoners. They'll arrange to kill me, and you'll get some official letter saying, 'We regret to inform you.'"

"Shut up!" he said. "Shut up and listen to me. Don't be on the defensive. Hit these guys at every opportunity—try to instill the fear of God in them."

"But, Dad, there's like a hundred of them."

"Then you've got a hundred shots to their one. Stay away from them? No, you do the opposite—you attack them. Throw them off balance. They're declaring war on you? Hell no! You declare war on them!"

I knew the odds were stacked to the moon against me, yet my dad's take on it somehow bolstered me. He made it sound like it just might be possible to survive. I clung to every word he said like it was the word of God.

As I felt my young life slipping away, I was not only terrified but infuriated. I had not started this. I wasn't bothering anyone when they brought this to me. And because I had the nerve to fight back, they were trying to kill me?

It's a horrifying feeling to know people are plotting to kill you. Out on the streets, I always had to be on the lookout for kids trying to beat me up. But there's a big difference between a few hard punches and murder. In this prison, it was life or death, and no in-between. Maybe they would get me in the end. Maybe I'd never get out of here, but I reminded myself of my promise: *I'm not going down without a fight.* My anguish and disappointment morphed into anger, an anger that hardened into pure hatred. I would take my father's advice and attack them. I would become a wolf. Woe unto my enemies.

Two days later, I was taken to the hole to serve my five days. "Hole time," also known as "lockdown" or, more formally, "solitary confinement," meant confinement to a cell for twenty-three hours a day, with one hour out for "rec." While serving my hole time, I received a gift from Old Folks just like the first time, only these two sheets of steel were already sharpened. Once again, I hid them in my mattress.

After my hole time was complete, I was returned to the cellhouse, but was moved to a different tier where Greg Larson resided, along with a guy named Claude Theriault, who would soon be on trial for his life. For some reason, I felt relatively comfortable around these two. They were older than I was, they were Independents, and they were both well respected. And they seemed okay with me, too. I minded my own business, never backed down from a fight, and held my mud. Claude was French Canadian, and in his distinct twang, he told me one day, "Frank, you're a good motherfucker."

I sensed that Greg and Claude were in my corner, and though they were both capable fighters, because of Pat McKenna's decree, which extended to every single person in the Nevada State Prison, they could never help me in a fight. But they did alert me to a BMF gangbanger's arrival on the tier. But I already knew; he and I had come face to face on the tier, where he'd smiled, fashioned his hand into a gun, pointed it at me, and popped the trigger. I calmly walked back to my cell and checked the handle on my knife. I would take my father's advice.

I laid awake most of the night, but by morning, I was ready. I would get him before he got me. Down from the culinary, past the sergeant's office, was a blind spot. After breakfast, I stood by the stairwell and waited. He was a big, muscled guy, and he came out of the culinary sort of slow, not expecting anything. As soon as he saw me, he reached for his shank. But it was too late. I moved in fast and stabbed him twice. He crumpled to the floor, while everyone, including me, scattered. He survived, although his injuries required surgery. He obviously knew exactly who'd stabbed him, but he held his mud. Though he said nothing to prison officials, the BMF would now come at me with everything they had.

As I prepared for their attacks, my senses became keener. I developed an acute peripheral vision, which became a natural part of my sight. I avoided blind spots and was always on high alert. I dared not let my guard down—not for one second. At night, I slept on top of my blankets—never under them. Getting twisted up in blankets could mean seconds that might cost me my life in an attack. I protected myself in every way I could think. I slept with my head away from the bars and put up a barrier between my bunk and the bars to protect my feet from being speared. Next, I fashioned a corset out of old *National Geographic* magazines I found lying around. The stiff cover and thickness of the magazine would protect my vital organs. I secured them around my back and abdomen using a bedsheet, tying them tightly to my body. Whenever danger was near, it seemed I got some kind of warning, like someone was whispering my name—*Frank* . . . Then everything seemed to slow down, as though moving in slow motion, and I knew something was about to jump off.

Within the first year of that early morning tier attack when four guys came toward my cell, knives in hand, I survived three more knife attempts on my life. Each encounter was one of intense violence that seemed to last forever but, in reality, was over in about a minute. After every battle, with adrenaline still pumping hard, I returned to my cell in a frenzy, squeezing my arms and flexing my fingers. *I'm alive! I'm alive.* When my body finally calmed, I fell quiet, sinking deeper into a rage-filled state. I no longer smiled; I never relaxed. Each day was life or death. There was nothing to smile about.

Each time I was attacked, I marked it on my cell wall with slashes. If I was moved to a different cell, the first thing I did was scrape the slashes onto the cement wall. I would never lose track. Out at the weight bench, I was lifting 250 pounds by this time, and when I wasn't pressing ever-increasing amounts of weight, I was shadowboxing and doing endless push-ups, sit-ups, and any other strength-building exercise I could think of. Faced with impossible odds, I needed every edge I could to stay one step ahead of my enemies. I didn't know how long it would be before they got me, but I couldn't think about it. I just had to keep trying to stay alive. One day at a time.

But my battles weren't always with the BMF. One evening, around dusk, I was walking alone through the yard. I turned the corner into a lonely stretch and stopped short. A bunch of gangbangers were circling a lone member of the Native American gang, the Tribe, readying to kill him. Pack mentality at its finest. I recognized him as a guy named Red Wolf. I wished I'd taken a different route, but I hadn't. I'd always had a deep sense of right and wrong, and this pack mentality just wasn't right.

I felt for my knife handle in my waistband and ran up to Red Wolf's side. He greeted me with a cheery thought, "Hey, Frank! Good day to die. Every day a good day to die. Today good day to die."

"Yeah, well, let's hope today's not that day, Red Wolf. At least not without a fight."

The attackers were crouching, and my heart was pounding. I just hoped Red Wolf would focus more on fighting than on the great beyond. But before anything jumped off, the side doors to the cellhouse opened and the Tribe spilled out—en masse. Fists were lowered, shanks disappeared, and the gang disbursed. I was greatly relieved.

A few days later, a ranking Tribe member told me the Tribe wanted to honor me for coming to Red Wolf's defense. He invited me to their sweat lodge, which was inside a teepee out by the old quarry on the prison grounds. The sweat lodge was a religious accommodation to the Native American prisoners. In general, prison officials tended to be leery of the Tribe. One time, the administration came out with a new prisoner hygiene policy that prohibited beards, required facial hair to be neatly trimmed, and mandated that hair be kept short. For the Native Americans, long hair was an essential part of their identity, so this new policy did not sit well with them.

After an afternoon spent drinking pruno, the convicts' home-made wine, emboldened Tribe members voiced their displeasure by abducting a sergeant, throwing a noose around his neck, and standing him on a desk and threatening to pull it out from under him unless the policy was rescinded. It was torn up immediately. The sergeant was released unharmed, and there was never any further talk about grooming standards.

I arrived at the teepee at the appointed time, where I was greeted by Chipmunk, the Tribe leader. He ushered me up to a pile of hot rocks where everyone was seated in a circle. Someone kept pouring water on the rocks and the steam sizzled and rose up. Man, was it hot. Sweat poured off me.

Chipmunk produced two long wooden boxes and opened them to reveal red velvet casings, one holding a pipe and the other an eagle feather. He removed the pipe and, as we smoked some tobacco, Chipmunk said I'd done an honorable thing for one of their brothers. "You're a good man, Frank De Palma."

He then carefully lifted the feather from its case. Speaking in his native tongue, he lightly glanced my shoulder and my head with the sacred feather. "I would give it to you," he said, "but federal law only allows ownership of eagle feathers by Native Americans. So, I'm doing the next best thing, Frank—I'm making you an honorary eagle feather holder."

I felt very moved and honored by all of this, but I also felt very hot. I could see them smiling at each other, getting a kick out of my discomfort. They were used to this intense heat, but I was not. But I would be damned if I would let on about it. I kept a straight face throughout—albeit a sweat-soaked face.

When the ceremony ended, I was never so happy to get out of that tent. But knowing I had forged an unexpected alliance with the Tribe made for a satisfying walk back to the cellhouse.

Too bad that alliance was useless when it came to my day-to-day survival. While the Tribe may have liked me as an individual, they would never go against Pat McKenna's directives toward me. I was not to be assisted or protected in any way. For the Tribe to do so would invoke the wrath of a gang that was much larger and far more vicious.

CHAPTER 10

Invictus!

Throughout the 1970s, during most of my twenties, life at the Nevada State Prison was dominated by the Aryan Warriors. That storied midnight summit between Warden Carl Hocker and Pat McKenna was continually borne out by the gang's unfettered criminal activities. Casino nights rolled along with all manner of contraband on open display—wads of cash, illegal drugs, and cases of premium liquor, all brought in by guards on the take.

Aryan Warriors on the outside relayed stories of guards riding around town in high-end cars—vehicles well out of reach of a correction officer's salary. It seemed everyone was either in on it or looking the other way.

But when drug deals soured, as they invariably did, and when big money was owed on lost bets, deadly retribution followed. Aryan Warrior hit crews, abetted by guards, made late-night cell door visits. "Suicides" were common, bodies piled up, and no one questioned it. Nobody cared. Hocker's famous words, "As long as my officers go home safe," were alive and well long after he was gone. Nothing else mattered.

The gang's reach and brutality were all-encompassing. As always, the hated snitch was ferreted out and dealt with viciously. I was in a corridor one night when a couple of Warriors led an ashen-faced con named Kevin Parker down the tier. Parker was scheduled to testify against one of the gang members. His name was on a witness list that a crooked lawyer must have leaked. As they passed by, I looked away, but I could make out their words to him, "You know what time it is, don't you?"

I turned back to see the guy nod.

The next morning, I awakened to what had become a familiar early morning announcement: "We got a hanger! We got one hanging."

I'd become largely desensitized to death, accustomed to pools of blood that were as common as puddles of rainwater, deaf to ungodly cries in the night that went unheeded. But Kevin Parker's murder got to me. I was haunted by the image of his resigned face. Why didn't he fight? Why didn't he lift a finger to defend himself? Seeing how I could never go down without a fight, this was something I would never understand.

Life inside the prison was marked by unimaginable depravity. The negativity that engulfed it seemed to have an evil life force itself, an energy that left nothing untouched. Even the wild animals that prowled the grounds were affected by it. Feral cats regularly made their way in and out of the prison, passing through the bars in search of a few scraps of food. One cat in particular, "Big Head," a rather large cat, was a mean one. He was called Big Head because, though he tried, his head was just too big to fit between the bars of the cells.

One afternoon, while we were confined inside for the count, somebody shouted, "Look! Big Head's done." We ran to the tier windows to glimpse a huge owl swooping down over the yard, Big Head in his sights. The owl sunk his talons into the cat, trying to fly off with his prey. He had a hard time pulling Big Head up, but then he got him, actually gaining height, flying him up and over the yard. It didn't look good for Big Head, but that cat was a fighter. He reached a paw up and got one of the owl's wings, and the owl started faltering. Big Head never lost his cool. He reached up and got the other wing. The cat and the owl came crashing to the ground, with Big Head on top. That cat tore into the bird's throat and killed him. Then he took the remains of the owl into his mouth and paraded him around the yard, making these loud, crazy growls. The convicts banged at the windows, yelping and cheering for Big Head. The other cats ran for cover. Nobody would mess with Big Head.

As I continued to fight back against the forces that were circling me, I saw Big Head as an inspiration. The slashes on my wall had notched up to ten, though not all of them represented actual combat. In one case, a BMF gangbanger brandished his shank and tried to take me out in the laundry area. But as soon as he glimpsed my weapon, which was bigger and sharper, he dropped his knife and took off. I didn't chase after him; there was no need. It would not go well for him when he tried to explain to his people why one of us wasn't dead.

But he'd shown me a knife, representing a threat to my life. I marked it on the wall. It counted.

Fighting or preparing for fights consumed me. One of the worst things about being targeted for death was not knowing when or from where the next attack was coming. I kept my mind sharp and my knives sharper. And as always, I was fanatical about my exercise regimen, combining the weight bench with hundreds of sit-ups, chin-ups, burpees, and anything else I could think of.

But I needed more for my image. My eye turned toward the tattoos worn by so many of the convicts. I'd never had any interest in tattoos before, but the idea was growing on me. I needed to appear as scary as I could to my enemies. I'd watched others applying homemade tattoos and decided to try it for myself. To create the ink, I burned some carbon paper and mixed it with water. Then I took a few straightened paperclips and sharpened them into needles by scraping them against the cement floor. Dipping them into the homemade ink, I went to work. I was no artist, but I managed to ink in a few dark skulls on my forearms. And it worked. The tattoos made me look a lot bolder than what I truly felt.

But my boldness wasn't all smoke and mirrors. I actually was becoming bolder, something I realized in a surprise encounter with none other than Pat McKenna himself. A few years had passed since that fateful yard encounter, and McKenna had never again directly acknowledged me. But when we ran into each other coming in from the yard one evening, he stopped and smirked. "You know," he said, "I should have just had you killed right from the start, instead of dragging it out with all of these fights."

In that moment, I knew for certain what I'd always suspected—that he'd engineered that rape attempt. His plan was to first degrade me and then watch me twist in the wind all alone before dying in a fight.

I pulled up my shirt to reveal my shank. "Or, how about *I* kill you right now?"

He jumped back, surprised, his hands feeling for a knife he wasn't carrying. He glanced around for his crew, but everyone had gone in. I caught a flicker of fear in the great Warrior's eyes. He was suddenly vulnerable—just like anybody else—and he knew it. "No, no, that's not what I'm saying. We're cool, man, we're cool."

Yeah, we were cool all right. I wasn't afraid of him anymore, nor was I overly concerned that he would issue an order to have me killed by one of his own. His efforts to destroy me had backfired. He thought he would have a little sick fun with me, but what he didn't bargain for was that I was surviving. I was supposed to have been dead by now. And every attack I walked away from garnered greater respect in a culture that valued toughness and violence above all else. I was making a name for myself as a fearsome, lone fighter. For him to rub me

out at this point for successfully defending my life would not
go over well, and he knew it.

"No, we're cool," he repeated, walking backwards away
from me, keeping his eye on my knife.

"Yup," I said.

By now, I was gaining respect from all quarters, including
the prison's old-timers. With their fighting days behind them,
these elderly cons were living out their final years on a quiet,
more secluded tier. One of them, a toothless old man, tottered
over to me in the yard and, with quivering fingers, handed me
a piece of paper with a poem written on it by someone named
William Ernest Henley. He said the poem reminded him of me
and told me I could keep it.

The poem was titled "Invictus," and as I read the words, I
got very excited. I felt like the poem was speaking to me.

Invictus

> Out of the night that covers me,
>   Black as the pit from pole to pole,
> I thank whatever gods may be
>   For my unconquerable soul.
>
> In the fell clutch of circumstance
>   I have not winced nor cried aloud.
> Under the bludgeonings of chance
>   My head is bloody, but unbowed.
>
> Beyond this place of wrath and tears
>   Looms but the Horror of the shade,
> And yet the menace of the years
>   Finds and shall find me unafraid.

> It matters not how strait the gate,
>> How charged with punishments the scroll,
> I am the master of my fate,
>> I am the captain of my soul.

I read it again and again, feeling infused with a greater strength, a sense of invincibility. *I am the master of my fate, I am the captain of my soul—yes!* I held on to that piece of paper, memorizing its words. It fortified me. It spurred me on. It became a part of me. *Invictus!*

CHAPTER 11

A Helicopter Built by Prisoners— "Hell Yeah!"

I was making a name for myself as a fighter, and it was noted not only by the convicts but by the prison officials. Consequently, I found myself doing a lot of hole time as punishment. But being locked down for twenty-three hours a day didn't really bother me; it was never more than the standard twenty-nine days straight, and I still got to go outside for that one hour of recreation, although not to the main yard but to a more secure, caged bullpen, where I was held alone.

But if this isolation was meant to deter me from fighting, it didn't work. I kept right at it, striking out often and hard, frantically trying to hold my enemies at bay. My life was at stake. The offensive strategy my father had instilled in me was working. But prison officials saw it differently, of course. To them, I was becoming a problem. Their solution was to transfer me out of the cellhouse, away from general population to a more secure unit known as "max housing."

Max housing, separated from the main cellhouse by a couple of security gates, was a two-story structure comprised of four 24-man cellblocks. Of its four cellblocks, one of them was death row, where the condemned awaited execution. The other three housed the most dangerous and incorrigible prisoners at the Nevada State Prison. At twenty-four years old, this was my new home. In the span of five short years, I had changed from a scared but hopeful teen into an enraged and violent young man.

Max housing was far more restrictive than the cellhouse. We were locked down for twenty-three hours a day. We did not go to the culinary for meals; food trays were delivered to our cells. Every other day, we were cuffed, shackled, and walked to an outside pen for recreation. There were usually five or six others in the pen, which allowed for a little socializing.

As I eked out an existence inside this somber housing unit, unbeknownst to me, the only rules I'd known inside the prison were starting to change. The seat of power, which had always resided with the gangs, was shifting, something I rudely discovered one afternoon while I was headed out for rec. After I'd been cuffed and shackled, a guard escorted me to the bullpen. When we got to the gate, I saw not only one, but several BMF members inside. And they saw me. I was badly outnumbered, and my heart started pumping hard. I could have asked the guard to take me back, but I didn't because that would have shown fear, and I could never allow that. If they smelled fear, I was done. Or maybe, if I had allowed myself to cave into it, I would have lost the nerve that was keeping me alive.

The guard removed the leg irons and unlocked the gate. But before he got to the cuffs, my enemies moved in on me. Predictably, the guard turned and ran away. Still handcuffed, I scrambled about, trying to kick them as hard as I could. But one of them got in close to me with something in his hand, and I felt a sharp pain in the base of my neck. A shout came from the gun tower for everyone to drop to the ground—face down. Nobody did. No one paid much attention to the gun tower. They stayed out of our business, and we stayed out of theirs. But this time was different. A warning shot was fired. My enemies dropped. I did not. If I went down, I wouldn't be able to see them. Still cuffed, blood streaming from my neck, I kicked and stomped them to keep them from getting up and attacking me again.

The gun tower guard trained his shotgun, and in one blast,

pumped me with birdshot. The force of it threw me to the ground, knocking me senseless. I heard whistles in the distance, followed by shouts into radios, and then felt the sensation of a stretcher beneath me as my shocked, bloody body was carted off to the infirmary. Though I was bleeding heavily from the birdshot, the doctor was more concerned about my neck. X-rays revealed something lodged inside. The doctor said it was a very delicate area near my spine and the object needed to be removed with precision. He extracted what turned out to be the long barrel of a pen. He told me I was very lucky; if I had been stabbed a hair closer to my spinal cord, I would have been paralyzed or dead.

He continued to examine my stomach, legs, and right hip, all heavily sprayed with birdshot and still oozing blood. I was enraged. This birdshot assault did not come from the BMF, but from the guards, the ones who'd always left us alone in exchange for their own safety. This was a betrayal. The laws we lived by had been broken. The guard who'd escorted me to the bullpen took off when I desperately needed his protection. That was part of the old deal, and I understood that. But now, the rules were changing. I would adjust. If the guards were coming at me, I would come at them. Putting hands on guards resulted in injuries that took a long time to heal. But I was so angry, I did not care. I would get that tower guard who shot me.

I bided my time, waiting for my moment. A couple of weeks later, I ran into him in a hallway. He looked at the floor and shuffled his feet when he saw me. "I'm glad to see you're doing okay," he said.

"Yeah, I'm okay," I answered, my chin up, my cheeks growing hot with anger. "But you're not."

I punched him square in the face. And then I didn't stop punching. My rage unleashed in a torrent of blows until other guards pulled me off him. I was immediately hauled off to the hole, and there was talk that I might face additional charges. I didn't care about additional charges. I didn't expect to live much longer anyway. What did it matter?

Although nothing came of the charges, that attack left me with new and extremely dangerous enemies—the guards. This was the first time I had laid my hands on a guard, but after that, it was on. The night after I was returned to max housing from the hole, at around 3:00 a.m., I heard movement on the tier. Before the footsteps reached my cell, I was on my feet. My cell gate popped open and five guards in black hoods rushed in and laid me out. I managed to yank the hoods off two of them and see their faces. I would get them both.

The following morning, I was splashing cold water on my swollen face when a voice from a few cells down called out to me, "Hey, man—you OK? They got you pretty good last night. I'm stringing up a line here. Let me send you down a few items."

Minutes later, I was pulling in coffee, a few cigarettes, and some foil covered chocolates. Those guards had really put a hurt on me, and these little treats lifted my spirits. As did this guy who sent them. He said his name was David Wayne. "But everybody calls me Bang-Bang. I guess I have a talent for bringing in guns," he laughed.

Bang-Bang was quite a talker, and just listening to his chatter distracted me from the pummeling I'd received. A couple of others also chimed in.

"Hey! How you doing, man?" asked a guy named Incel Ball, a round, jolly sort who struck me as being out of place in prison.

A little further down the tier, a tall guy with long dark hair leaned on his bars and said to me, "The way you go after the guards? You're one crazy motherfucker. But I like you." He said his name was Allen Taylor.

As I got to know them, I learned that Allen was part Native American and part French Canadian. A quiet intellectual, he read books like *War and Peace* and *Crime and Punishment*. He was also a good fighter, but that wasn't exactly what had landed him in max housing. Allen had a penchant for bringing credible and frequent lawsuits against the Department of Prisons. Viewed as a troublemaker, he was kept where they could keep a close eye on him.

Incel was a good-natured guy who didn't want to hurt others or cause problems. To him, life was a party, and everybody should just have a good time. He avoided violence, but if threatened, he did not walk away, as one disrespectful prisoner had learned when Incel clobbered in his head with a pipe, resulting in his transfer to max housing.

The four of us were close in age and got creative in communicating, fashioning lines known as "cadillacs" that allowed us to pass each other "kites," which were basically notes, as well as coffee and other necessities. We made lines using torn strips of sheet tied down with old shampoo bottles or whatever might have enough weight to be thrown down the tier. Although we weren't friends, per se, as there were no real friendships in prison, I'd have to say a certain camaraderie developed among the four of us.

David "Bang-Bang" Wayne, thanks to his gun capers, was well known at the prison. A real character, he had pals everywhere. One of them was a guy named Jesse Bishop, who I bumped into in the infirmary one day. "Hey," he said. "You're Bang's friend."

Bishop was rather dashing, always a cigar in hand. With a black mustache and an easy smile, he appeared to have not a care in the world. I asked him how he was doing, and he shrugged. "You know, waiting, that's all, man. Just waiting." He made it sound like he was waiting for a bus.

But what the forty-six-year-old was waiting for was his execution. He had given up his appeals on a murder conviction and sat on death row, resigned to an approaching date with the Nevada gas chamber.

On October 22, 1979, that date came, and the outside world turned its attention to the Nevada State Prison. News reporters camped out on the grounds in the hours leading up to the execution in what could only be described as a circus-like atmosphere. Pointing their cameras up to the death house and joking around with prison officials, the media was having a grand old time. In contrast to the liveliness outside, the mood inside the prison was somber. Though violence and death were our constant companions, this was different. A man was about to lose his life in a lawful, calculated manner. Every one of us convicts felt the gravity of it. Yes, Jesse Bishop had killed someone, but he was also a former paratrooper, a decorated war hero, a man who had lost his way. Like so many others in here.

Just after midnight, Jesse Bishop was put to death by cyanide gas. He would be the last person in Nevada to be executed by this method.

Shortly thereafter, Claude Theriault, the Canadian guy who had befriended me before I was moved to max housing, who had told me I was "a good motherfucker," lost his capital murder case. He packed up his belongings and was escorted to a cell on death row.

That same year, Pat McKenna, my chief nemesis, would strangle his cell mate. Though he would remain in the general population through decades of appeals and new trials, in the end, the invincible shot caller himself would also take his place on death row.

Such was life at the Nevada State Prison. Though most prisoners were not facing execution, they were living a day-to-day life that was slow and torturous—a death sentence, nonetheless. With many facing life without parole, and with nothing to look forward to beyond endless boredom and despair, thoughts naturally turned to escape.

Perhaps the boldest attempt at freedom was a 1982 effort to build a helicopter and fly it up and over the yard and gun towers, saying farewell to it all. Using a motorcycle engine and lawn mower blades, it was assembled in an outside maintenance area. The project was quite sophisticated but was discovered before it could have been tested. The audacity of a homemade helicopter at the prison put the novel venture on the evening news, which is how most of us found out about it. Although it did not succeed, just the idea of it energized the place. A helicopter built by prisoners! "Hell yeah!" Newscasters said if it hadn't been discovered, it might have had a shot. But even if the helicopter never lifted up and over the prison, it surely did lift our spirits.

But like the failed helicopter escapade, most escape plans were nothing more than pipe dreams. The more common escape was losing oneself through drugs, something I religiously avoided. There was no way I would get into the drug scene. I had to be alert at all times, and I attributed my survival, at least in part, to refraining from drug use. "Get high and die" was my personal motto. Though I never indulged, drugs were everywhere, and drug-induced euphoria was commonplace. But when it wore off, the same miserable reality awaited. The only true escape was death, making suicide a reasonable option. The usual method of ending one's life was through an overdose. Intentional overdoses were common. When someone made the decision to end it, the unwritten law among the prisoners was to refrain from interfering. *Let him go, let him be free.*

While I understood the appeal of suicide, I also recognized that my situation was a little different. I did not have a life sentence. If I managed to survive these knife attacks and didn't pick up any additional charges, there was still the chance I could be out in a few years and this whole nightmare could be over with. Deep within my ever-hardening heart, a ray of hope still flickered. I sought to banish it, of course, as I needed to stay firmly focused. But hope isn't easily vanquished. I added more ugly tattoos to my arms and, in a rare slip into hopefulness, I asked a fellow convict to ink one word on my back for me: *Vivien*.

CHAPTER 12

Hypocrisy, Corruption, and the Fall of the Status Quo

That birdshot attack on me was just one incident in a growing wave of encroachments on the prisoners. But just as the encroachments began, they inexplicably receded, and life at the Nevada State Prison was back to business as usual. The Aryan Warriors did their thing, and the guards joined them or looked the other way. Just as long as there were no escapes and the officers went home unharmed, everyone was content.

But in 1980, it all blew up when a guy named Danny Jackson was found hanging in the old cellhouse yard shower. That familiar early morning cry, "We got a hanger," should have been like any other hanging, no big deal. Except in this case, Jackson's family demanded to see the body, which was most unusual. Deep ligature marks were found around his wrists, indicating he had been bound; it was obvious he couldn't have hanged himself. It was murder, and the shock of it made the newspapers.

Overnight, the prison administration went nuts. Top brass were running around the place, barking orders and shouting into walkie-talkies. The casino was shut down, and this time for good. High-ranking heads rolled, resignations followed, and new policies hit the prison like a tsunami. Aggressive efforts to ferret out weapons became the sudden new norm, which meant regular pat-downs and cell searches.

Two Aryan Warriors were subsequently charged and convicted of murdering Danny Jackson.

But the new security measures went beyond pat-downs and cell searches. The prison administration's corruption had been exposed, and they were on an angry mission, unleashing their fury on us. They announced they would be confiscating all our personal belongings, presumably to inspect them for hidden weapons. Cell by cell, guards made their way through the entire prison, taking what little we had. The tiers were quickly filling up with TVs, framed photos, and little gifts sent by our families. When they got to my cell, they took the only thing I owned, the radio my dad had sent me years earlier. I still listened to it in the evenings. There was nothing inside. I asked them to unscrew the back of it right then and there and check for weapons. But they refused, telling me I'd get it back if it was clean.

We all watched helplessly as guards carted off our meager possessions. I felt especially bad for a guy named Sluggo, a member of the Mexican gang, *Mi Raza Unida*. He'd been so happy and proud the day his TV arrived, a gift from his family. They had chipped in and scraped up enough to buy it for him. Now, all he could do was stand by helplessly as it was taken away.

Contrary to assurances that everything would be returned once it was checked over, not one item was ever brought back. Prisoners who worked outside details reported seeing our belongings being thrown into the back of a dump truck, with the guards helping themselves to whatever they wanted. In the weeks that followed, we kept asking about our stuff. At first, they said nothing, and then they told us everything had been destroyed by a flood in the basement. We all knew it was bullshit.

This blatant theft left me with an even colder hatred toward our keepers, the ones who were supposed to be better than us. Some of the guards who were now patting us down and searching our cells were the very same ones bringing in drugs, taking payoffs, and opening cell doors for gang hit crews. The hypocrisy of it all was sickening, and I fought them at every turn with everything I had.

As my reputation for battling the guards grew, I became one of their prime harassment targets. One guard, a guy named Smitty, a real smart-ass, sauntered up to my cell and smirked. "You know, De Palma, one of these days I'm going to beat your ass."

I reached through the bars and grabbed him. "Yeah, how about now?"

He broke away but stumbled backward and fell on his ass. I laughed at him. A little while later, he returned with three guards. While he stood outside, they unlocked and slid open my barred cell door and rushed in. My adrenaline was pumping hard, and I landed a few good ones. But at three against one, their favored ratio, I got whooped. I didn't care. I licked my wounds, lifted more weights, and readied to go at it with them again at the first opportunity.

And so it went. I no longer distinguished between the prisoner blues and the tan uniforms. They were all the same to me. They were all my enemies. If their intent was to subdue me, it had the opposite effect. I was young, strong, and enraged, and I would fight them morning, noon, and night.

By now, I was a permanent resident in max housing. If I wasn't in my cell, then I was doing hole time. Every effort was being made to control me, and nothing was working.

I had just completed another ten days of hole time, and I was waiting for the max sergeant to escort me back to my cell. But instead of a sergeant appearing, two guards showed up and told me the warden wanted to talk to me. I knew something wasn't right. They escorted me, handcuffed and shackled, through the main control gate, where we passed the barbershop and headed up to the muster room, the large space where the guards stood for roll call between shifts. As soon as we entered the muster room, I knew everything was wrong. Before me stood six or so guards, along with the prison doctor, standing there in his long white coat. To his side was a little nurse with a big syringe in her hand. She looked quite frightened.

The doctor told me I was being taken someplace better than the Nevada State Prison and that he was going to give me something to calm my nerves and help me relax a little. I had no intention of going along with being injected with God knows what was in that syringe. I smiled politely and said, "Thank you, doctor." I told a guard to take the nurse away. Then I launched myself at the doctor.

We both went to the floor, and I struggled with him, which is all I really could do because of the shackles and manacles. As we thrashed about, someone kept trying to jab me with the needle, but it kept breaking as I twisted every way I could to avoid it. Finally, somebody grabbed a plank of wood and got me with a hard blow to the head. My head exploded in white light.

CHAPTER 13

Primum non nocere

I will rocket your brain to Mars.
—DR. ROBERT FRANCIS FREEMAN

When I opened my eyes, I was on the floor of some room that looked entirely unfamiliar. I could barely raise my head, it hurt so bad. I was also groggy, as though I'd been drugged. I had been transported to the psychiatric ward of the Northern Nevada Correctional Center for reasons I did not yet understand.

I lay in a cell in that stupor-like state for several days. When I started to come around, I learned that three other prisoners from max housing had joined me in nearby cells—Allen Taylor, Incel Ball, and David Wayne. The four of us had been placed under the care of medical chief and psychiatrist Dr. Robert Francis Freeman, who began injecting us with a cocktail of psychiatric medications, starting with Prolixin, a powerful antipsychotic medication used to treat serious disorders such as schizophrenia. None of us had schizophrenia or any other type of psychiatric disorder, for that matter. There had never been a request for our consent. It didn't matter. David received one shot of Prolixin, Allen got two or three, and Incel received four or five.

I, on the other hand, received Dr. Freeman's special attention. He injected me not only with Prolixin but also with Thorazine and Haldol, heavy-duty medications for severe psychiatric disorders. The effects of these drugs on my brain were devastating. My mind simply went blank in a way I had never experienced before. It was terrifying. I couldn't put a thought together. There was just nothing. After what I can only surmise must have been a few days of lying on my bunk in this blank state, I was able to slowly start piecing thoughts together again, and as I started coming back, I was furious at what had been done to me.

But this was just the beginning. No sooner had I started to feel like my normal self than Freeman was at my door, another big needle in hand. He ordered me to "present" my arm in the door slot for another injection.

"Fuck you!" I shouted at him.

He repeated his demand. I repeated my response.

He smiled and disappeared. About ten minutes later, he returned, along with several guards, one of them carrying a 12-gauge beanbag shotgun, which was a powerful stun gun with enough force to break a man's ribs. "Now," he said, "you will present your arm."

I was on my feet. "Fuck you!"

One of the guards said, "We're giving you one more warning. Move up to the slot and put your arm out."

"I never agreed to this!" I shouted. "No!"

They swung the cell door open, and a guard leveled the gun at me. I tried to run this way and that, but trapped in the small space, there was nowhere to go. He fired. *Boom!* If a major league pitcher had thrown his best fast ball directly into my chest, it wouldn't have matched the power of the gun. It knocked me down, and I writhed on the floor. While I struggled to pull air into my lungs, Freeman rushed in and jabbed me with the needle. Once again, I fell unconscious.

About a week later, I had once again rallied, but there he was, demanding that I present my arm. Once again, I refused. This time the guards were with him, and my door was quickly unlocked, and I was fired upon. *Bam!* Those bean bag shots got the best of me, leaving me on the floor, gasping for air and covered in rings of purple bruises that extended from my chest down to my groin. I was so sore, and I later learned that these guns should never be fired at close range. After the third time they blasted me, there was no struggle left in me. The next time Freeman showed up at my door, I dutifully presented my arm for another megadose of his diabolical concoction.

"Why?" I asked him. "Why are you doing this to me?"

He smiled. "My orders are to break you by any means necessary. If I have to, I'll rocket your brain to Mars."

So, these were the measures the Nevada Department of Prisons would take to control me, and this Freeman guy was their man to do it. I knew how to fight with my fists, but against these injections, I was defenseless.

As the weekly regimen continued, I lost all sense of time, all connections to reality. I was losing my mind, and there was nothing I could do about it. Those drugs took away my will, my energy, my fight. In a routine that would go on for five months, Freeman would show up at my cell each week, a barely contained look of joy on his face. "Mr. De Palma, how are we feeling today?" With his goatee and sinister smile, I thought he looked like the devil himself. Occasionally, I spat a good one in his face. For that, he'd return sooner with another fat dose.

After the injections, my body would shake badly. Freeman never bothered with medication to offset the side effects of these powerful drugs. My teeth chattered and my jaw twisted from side to side, locking up on one side. I felt like there were a billion ants crawling in my stomach. As I fought against the ants and tried to unlock my jaw, I shuffled and paced the cell endlessly, so much so that my feet blistered and bled. It was that way for all four of us. Allen Taylor left footprints of blood on his way to the shower. I later learned this shuffling had a name—the "Prolixin shuffle." I was in a horrible way, mentally and physically. We all were.

Sometimes, while in this blank-minded state, I would get a flash, a jolt that caused an involuntary muscle jerk, a flinch that seemed to bring a single word into my brain: "Me." Another flash would bring another word: "Frank." *Frank, me.* I would try to hold on to that. Then other flashes would come, giving me more to build on, which brought me back to awareness. *Yes, I am Frank. I am me. I am alive.* The flashes, the jolts, grew in intensity, and I likened it to a power grid that had lost all power but was slowly coming back online. It was my power grid coming back up. My brain. My brain's synapses were firing again, restoring me back to function.

But how long could I hold on to this function? How long could I hold on to myself? Just when I thought I had it back together, my brain would suddenly go blank again—with or without the shots. I worried that the next shutoff might be permanent. Would I be discovered lying there unblinking, unmoving, only to have some prison doctor diagnose me as being catatonic, in some persistent vegetative state, in need of care for the rest of my life? Would I be lost to everything, everyone, including myself, except that I might, on some very primal level, know that I existed?

Though prison had taken away all my freedoms, it had never occurred to me that my mind could also be taken. Through the fog of these drugs, I knew I had to do something. No one told us how long this was going to last, and fearing it might never end, in my semi-lucid moments, especially just prior to the next injection, I did some hard thinking. How could I take the chance that my brain would continue to turn on? Was it my spirit, my will that brought me back from nothingness to being? Was my spirit strong enough to keep bringing me back to awareness, to the living? Or would it eventually give out? Given the choice between a gun to shoot myself in the head and another injection, I can honestly say that I would have grabbed the gun. I would rather have died than lain there with no control of my very being. If I was dead, then I wouldn't have to worry, to fear that I would become a vegetable.

I did not have access to a gun, but when another type of opportunity presented itself, I took it. In between the injections, as the drugs' effects were wearing thin, I spoke with an inmate psych attendant named Jimmy. He told me he was ready to check out, that he was depressed, miserable, and saw no point in living. He told me he was expecting a delivery of quaaludes and that he had every intention of overdosing. I asked him if there would be enough for two.

"Are you sure?" he asked.

I told him yes, that I was done. I would rather be dead than endure another minute of this. I was ready to go to sleep and never wake up. My life would be over at twenty-four years old, but I didn't see any other way.

He agreed to split the drugs with me. He wasn't exactly sure when they would be smuggled in, but figured it was a matter of days. I felt a sense of great relief. The ants, the twisted jaw, the bleeding feet, the insanity—it would all be over soon.

Later in the week, I was just waking when Allen, who was in the cell next to me, yelled, "Hey, Frank! Jimmy's gone."

"Where'd he go?"

"He's gone, gone. Dead. They just fished his body out of his cell."

I slumped back. What happened? I was supposed to have been gone, too. Why hadn't he given me any of the quaaludes? This horror show was supposed to be over. I punched the wall. He had not kept his word. *He'd promised!* When Freeman showed up at my door with his needle, I felt utterly hopeless. I couldn't even die to escape this.

In the next moment of semi-lucidity, while I was out of my cell for a trip to the shower, I spoke with Allen, David, and Incel. We all agreed that we needed to get somebody's attention. Someone had to listen—someone had to stop this. We kicked it around and decided our best shot was to grab a guard and hold him hostage—not to hurt him but to make it stop. It was drastic, but we couldn't think of any other way out of this. We were desperate.

And so, we hatched a plan. During one of my shower trips, Incel would beckon a guard to his cell to speak with him about something or other. Using a sharpened spoon handle that we would get from one of the inmate psych attendants, I would come up from behind and hold the spoon to his throat, demanding to speak to someone in charge.

We put our plan into motion quickly. With sharpened spoon handle in hand, we waited for the next guard to come by. Unfortunately, it was one of the more decent guards. As soon as I saw who it was, I almost had a change of heart. His name was Officer Kelly, but everybody called him "Radar," after the mild-mannered Radar O'Reilly on M*A*S*H.

But there was no turning back; Incel had already beckoned Radar to his cell, and I moved in fast, grabbing him around the neck. "I'm sorry it has to be you, Radar," I told him. "But we can't take this anymore."

With his head pressed against my shoulder, he said, "I know, Frank, I know. We see it. It's wrong, but there's nothing we can do."

"Something's going to get done now," I said. "I'm sorry it's you, Radar, I truly am. But if you fight me, I'll kill you. Don't struggle, Radar, please don't struggle."

In an instant, alarms were sounding, and guards were racing in. Allen knocked out the first two of them, and I was holding tight to Radar, desperate for a chance to plead our case. But then

Radar started struggling. "I told you, don't fight me! I told you!" He started thrashing, and we went to the floor. I straddled him and stabbed him in the chest. I tried to stab him again, but the handle on the spoon came off and I lost my grip, which is what probably saved his life. Guards were everywhere now, pulling him out from under me.

And then they rolled up on me. I braced myself for the customary beating, but nothing happened. They were suspiciously calm. This time they had something very different in mind. I was dragged into my cell, stripped naked, and held down on the floor and spread eagled. In a maneuver that must have been well thought out, they methodically wrapped gauze around my wrists and ankles, and then snapped handcuffs onto each wrist and ankle. The steel bunk had six holes in it, three on each side. Using belly chains, they wove the chains through the holes. Then someone said, "Get his ass under the bunk."

I was shoved underneath on my back and held up against the bottom of the bunk, with my arms outstretched over my head. The chain ends were then attached to the handcuffs.

"Okay, drop his ass."

And my body fell. The pain was immediate and excruciating. I was suspended underneath the bunk, my butt two inches from the floor. I felt the warmth of blood and intense pain in my wrists and ankles. And just like that, they locked up the cell and left me, naked and chained underneath the steel bed frame.

I hung there, in sheer agony, my wrists and ankles feeling like they were being pulled apart from the rest of me by my own weight. I hoped this would end quickly. But when I overheard instructions being given to another inmate psych attendant that he would be in charge of "feeding and watering" me, I knew it wasn't ending anytime soon. The pain was unbearable. My wrists and ankles were taking the brunt of it, and the slightest move on those joints was agony. I thought they would simply break off. My attempts to hold my head up to keep it from flopping back brought untold pain to my neck and back. Letting it fall back was no better, and I alternated between both positions as best I could. The pain got so bad that my brain would shut off, my body would shut off, and I would fall unconscious. When I came to, I was able to endure it for a couple more hours before the pain overwhelmed me, and I would lose consciousness again. Unconsciousness was my only relief.

Three times a day, the psych attendant, a guy named Billy Russell, crawled under the bed and shoved food in my mouth, followed by quick sips of water. He was allotted exactly two minutes to feed me. "Don't worry, Frank, I got you," he said.

Billy Russell had killed his wife and kids, which placed him among the lowliest of prisoners. I had hated him for this, but I didn't hate him anymore. Whenever I had to urinate or defecate, I simply did so, right on the floor. I had no choice. Despite the growing stench in my cell, Billy never once balked. He tended to me with kindness, never complaining about this horrible assignment, something I'll never forget. As the foul odor of the cell permeated out through the door, I had to listen to guards in the hall spewing the most profane, humiliating garbage at me on a constant basis.

But the foul smell and the sight of my tortured condition did not deter the good Dr. Freeman from coming in with the needle and jabbing me. But the stink and sight of me must have gotten to him, because after a couple more injections, even he backed off.

I dangled from the underside of that bunk for over three weeks—twenty-three days, to be exact. I don't know how I survived it. But it all came to an abrupt head when civilians from the outside stormed in. I don't know who they were, I only remember a lot of shouting and figures in windbreakers. My door was thrust open, where my condition was plain to see and smell. Everything blew up. I heard loud voices and some-one being ordered to uncut me. Whoever received the order complained about the piss and shit.

"I don't give a fuck!" was the answer. "Unchain him now."

A woman I did not recognize was looking in at me, sobbing. With what little energy I had, I whispered, "Get her out of here, please."

I don't remember much more than that as I was in a rather debilitated state. I vaguely recall plastic bags being placed under me. But I well remember the moment the chains were cut and the pressure was off. The relief was just so "oh, man." I was slid out from underneath the bunk, wrapped in sheets, and carried to a shower, where I remained under hot running water for a very long time.

In the aftermath of this horror, I learned that Dr. Robert Francis Freeman was not only a psychiatrist and chief of Nevada's prison medical services, but he was also a felon. Before turning to crime, he had been a medical doctor practicing psychiatry in Missouri, but his license had been revoked by the state. He had also served seven years in a maximum-security prison in Michigan for armed robbery. Unbelievable as that sounded, articles about him had appeared in the *Reno Gazette-Journal,* where prison director Charles Wolff acknowledged Freeman's criminal history, but defended his employment, saying, "Nevada's prison system is fortunate to have a full-time physician at all. It's difficult to get a full-time doctor at the salary we're paying."

For my part in stabbing Officer Kelly, I pleaded guilty to assault with a deadly weapon and received another three years to my growing sentence structure. I had neither the energy nor the mental clarity to defend myself or try to put my actions into the context of desperation and a drug-addled brain. I also felt bad about hurting Radar. Had the handle not come off that spoon, he might have died. He was one of the truly decent guards who treated everyone like they mattered. He just got caught up in a horribly desperate situation. At the hearing, despite the fact that I'd stabbed him, Officer Kelly actually stood up and decried the forced injections and the cruel acts that took place afterward. I deeply appreciated that.

Through secondhand sources, I was told that the nurse who drew up the massive medicine doses Freeman was ordering wound up being treated for the trauma she had suffered from all that she witnessed. I don't know if it's true, but it would not have surprised me.

Though I would pay my dues for my violent action, no one else would be penalized for theirs. The Nevada Department of Prisons was never held accountable for torturing me for those three weeks. Their own criminal behavior would be overlooked. They could do whatever they pleased, lawful or otherwise.

But regarding the forced medication, there was some justice. Washoe Legal Services filed a lawsuit on behalf of myself, Allen, and Incel. Unfortunately, I was dropped from the case as I was too mentally compromised to assist the attorneys with the litigation. I learned that the medication I'd been injected with can stay in the brain for months after stopping all use. It would be close to a year before I felt entirely free of the drugs' effects. Nonetheless, the lawsuit produced results. Allen and Incel each received a few thousand dollars, but more important, new laws were enacted to better protect prisoners against forced medication.

I have often wondered who it was that blew the whistle on the horrors inside the psych ward at the Northern Nevada Correctional Center, but I thank God for that person or persons. Rumor had it that it was actually a hard-nosed guard who'd seen enough and did something. Maybe.

But through the haze of it all, I distinctly remember one name: Kathleen Fogarty. I couldn't see her face or how she fit into this, yet her name stayed with me. Decades later, through sheer happenstance, I got to meet Kathleen Fogarty and learned that she had been there that day, working as a paralegal with Washoe Legal Services. She filled in many of the blanks, including conversations she'd had with Allen, David, and Incel, who'd also been "four-pointed" under the bunks, as she phrased it. She well remembers the horrible condition we were in. She also told me the details surrounding the forced injection lawsuit. It was all very validating. Her memory was so vivid and accurate, even forty years later. I had to ask her how she remembered all of this, to which she answered, "How do you forget?"

CHAPTER 14

Dashed Hopes

The most dangerous creation of any society
is the man who has nothing to lose.
—James A. Baldwin, *The Fire Next Time*

After the debacle at the Northern Nevada Correctional Center, David, Allen, Incel, and I were quietly returned to the Nevada State Prison. As the medications slowly drained from my brain and I fully regained my faculties, I was outraged at what had been done to me, both the forced medication and the torturous three weeks underneath that bunk. But more than being angry, I was terrified. What next? What would they do to me next? I had to get out of here. I wanted to escape this prison nightmare in the worst way.

So, one afternoon, when Bang-Bang pulled me to a secluded area of the yard to discuss an escape plan he was hatching, I was more than interested. What he had in mind was a breakout from the courtroom during his upcoming trial on an outstanding charge.

"Here's what I'm thinking," he whispered. "It'll be me, you, and Incel. I'll have the two of you added to my witness list as character witnesses, and you'll both be in the waiting room. I figure we'll need a couple of guns to bust out, which my girlfriend is getting. Once we're clear of the courthouse, she'll drive us to a switch car, and from there, we'll go to a rented safe house. Then we'll lay quiet for a couple of weeks."

As he laid it out, my pulse quickened. Knowing the courthouse layout as I did from personal experience, I thought we stood a pretty good chance of pulling it off. My mind started racing with possibilities. After the safe house, maybe I could move far away, to a quiet life somewhere else, perhaps a sandy beach in Mexico or the Caribbean—anywhere but this country and its horrible prisons.

"What do you think our odds are?" I asked him.

"I'd say fifty-fifty."

I thought about it for a moment, reflecting on the fact that I faced daily death threats from the BMF, was regularly beaten by guards, and had almost lost my mind at the Northern Nevada Correctional Center. I didn't have to think about it for long. Fifty-fifty odds were better than my odds of surviving this place. "Count me in."

A few months into 1981, our preparations were underway. Bang's girlfriend, Teree Lee, had smuggled two guns into the prison. Teree Lee and Bang-Bang reminded me of a modern-day Bonnie and Clyde. There was nothing she wouldn't do for Bang. Next, she secured our getaway and switch cars, complete with shotguns in case of a car chase. Everything was falling into place. I could practically smell the salty ocean air.

In early May, Bang-Bang began his proceedings, taking his legal papers to court where he and his attorney were preparing his defense. Concealed inside his paperwork were the guns. He dared not leave them in his cell for fear they'd be discovered in a random search. In the era before metal detectors, moving them in and out of the prison wasn't that problematic.

With Bang's trial date drawing closer, Incel and I were added to the witness list. The guns would be taped underneath the waiting room table where Incel and I could grab them. We would brandish the guns and the three of us would make a run for it. Teree Lee had secured the safe house. We were set.

As I mentally rehearsed the way it would go down, fear and panic were fast eclipsing my salty air fantasies. To burn off nervous energy, I did jumping jacks and countless burpees, push-ups, and sit-ups until my cell floor was covered with puddles of sweat. Any day now, Incel and I would be called into court. I was scared, but then again, fear had been my companion most of my life, and we got along just fine. In the end, I had nothing to lose.

The day before Bang-Bang's trial was to begin, I awoke early, as I usually did, listening as the rest of my confined world stirred to life. Breakfast came and went. I exercised. Lunch came and went. The day was passing as it did most every day: boringly slow. As I continued with my daily routine of exercise, cleaning, and pacing the tiny cell, I arrived at some unspoken understanding within myself, a sense of quiet calm. If the endeavor didn't work out, I would be okay with it.

It was late afternoon, and I was on my bunk watching cockroaches scurry across the wall when I heard shuffling footsteps nearby. Then I heard the gate of the empty cell next to me open, slide back, and lock shut. An instant later, Bang-Bang appeared, wearing his orange transports, unescorted and unshackled. Something was wrong. He opened his hand to reveal a small shiny gun—a .32 caliber Baretta, fully loaded.

Before I could open my mouth to speak, he gave me the "shhh" gesture with his finger. I whispered, "What the hell's going on, brother?"

He quietly told me that when he'd returned from court, one of the guards, a guy named Gifford, insisted on going through his paperwork. Every other day, the guards had only given his folders a cursory glance, but Gifford was filling in for somebody that day. "I tried to get him to back off, but all he did was get mouthy, so I told him I'd help him out. I pulled out one of the guns and pointed it at him."

My heart lurched. *Oh my God!*

"I had no choice! So, I handcuffed him and the other two."

"What other two?"

"Casselli and Davis. They were with Gifford." He motioned toward the cell next to me. "They're all in there. I had them cuff themselves to each other."

What?! I was growing hot with anger. This was a disaster.

"It's okay," Bang insisted.

I shook my head. "It's not okay! It's not okay, Bang! What the hell do we do now? What are we going to do when they come for us? And they'll come hard."

"If it looks like we're going down, we'll take out all three hostages. Have a little faith in my plan."

"What plan? This wasn't supposed to happen."

"Don't worry," he said. "Trust me. We'll figure it out."

My heart sank. There wasn't going to be any figuring this out. Still, Bang had been there for me, a rarity behind bars. I gave him my word I'd follow his lead.

He reached inside his waistband and pulled out the second gun—a .38-caliber, five-shot Smith & Wesson that undercover cops often keep on their ankle. It had a small handle, but it was a real gun with real bullets. Five of them. He handed it to me, but not before I agreed not to brandish it unless I had no choice and that if he asked for it back, I would give it to him. I lifted my shirt, quickly wrapped an ACE bandage around my waist, and secured the gun inside. Next was to get Incel out of his cell, take the hostages to the sergeant's office where there was a phone, and figure things out from there.

Using the brass keys he'd lifted from the guards, Bang unlocked my cell, and we went next door where three stone-faced guards sat on the steel bunk. I knew all three. There was

Officer Gifford, who was probably wishing he had been more decent to us. Gifford was one of those guards who hated convicts and was quick to let us know it. He and I had exchanged words in the past. I did not care for him at all and couldn't pass on the chance to mess with his head. "How ya' doing, Giff? You're looking a little pale. You okay?"

Bang-Bang was aware of my dislike for Gifford and gave me a nervous glance. I winked at him.

Then there was Mr. Casselli. He was young and new to the prison, but he was quiet, polite, and respectful to everyone. No one had any issues with him. Next was Officer Bucky Davis. He was an old-school guard. He minded his own business, did his job, gave us what we had coming, and gave respect to those who respected him. He never went out of his way to hassle others, but if trouble came his way, he wasn't one to back down.

Bang separated their handcuffs and re-cuffed them individually behind their backs. He told them he would place the cuffs in front once inside the sergeant's office. "But," he warned, "if any of you get stupid, I won't hesitate to shoot. Understand?"

All three nodded.

We marched the three of them out, and as we passed by the cells, the prisoners were at their bars, quietly taking it all in. Seeing a couple of convicts, one of them holding a semiautomatic pistol, walking three guards down the tier rendered them speechless. At least for the moment.

"Well, it took you guys long enough," Incel said when we reached his cell. "Let me out." I unlocked his gate; he came out and smirked at the hostages. "I hope you guys get overtime for this."

"Fat chance of that!" Officer Davis said.

As we headed to the sergeant's office, a few of the convicts asked Bang-Bang to let them out. He told them to hold on. Once inside the office, the guards were re-cuffed in front and seated on chairs lined against the wall. Bang sat down at the desk and called the main security post and asked for Captain Adam Blake, who was in charge that afternoon. By now, prison officials knew three guards had been taken hostage. I listened as Bang spoke to Blake: "The hostages are unhurt, and yes, I have a gun, but no one gets hurt as long as nobody gets heroic." He assured Blake that he would get verbal confirmation of good health from one of the guards soon. Then Bang made a request for drugs, specifically Demerol. He nodded in a way that told me Blake was agreeing to it.

Apparently, Blake had a request of his own, asking but one favor. "What's that?" Bang-Bang asked him. "Huh?" he said aloud. "Don't let De Palma out of his cell?" Bang's smile grew wide, and he handed me the phone. "It's for you."

I spoke into the phone. "Hello!"

Blake shouted, "De Palma's out of his cell!"

"Ah, shit!" I heard in the background.

"Don't hurt anyone," Blake said to me.

I said nothing and passed the phone back to Bang. He told Blake that I was the first one he let out, but that I was being cool. Bang gave Officer Davis the phone and ordered him to tell Blake that the three of them were unhurt. Then Bang got back on and told Blake he'd be waiting on the Demerol.

The prisoners were now clamoring to get out of their cells, the noise level rising on the tiers. Things were growing tense. Max housing held the most violent people in Nevada's prison system. Most were in here for life and had nothing to lose. Everyone carried weapons, and everyone had enemies inside here and would not hesitate to kill their enemies given the opportunity. This situation could easily turn into a bloodbath. Normally, the four tiers were released to the yard in separate shifts to avoid deadly confrontations—unless the guards felt like playing games, of course. We knew that violence among the prisoners could lead to panic by law enforcement, resulting in a deadly outcome.

"Let's just leave them locked in," Incel suggested, which was not a bad idea.

Bang disagreed. "We're going to let them out. Just not all at once. First, we'll unlock the cell doors, and they can come out onto the tiers. We'll see how that goes before we unlock the tier gates. But no one except the three of us comes into this office with the hostages. If any of these guards gets hurt or killed, there'll be lots of dead cons."

Bang turned and glared at Officer Gifford. "If Captain Blake or his friends get stupid, we'll throw you to the convicts."

Gifford stared straight ahead.

Incel stayed with the hostages while Bang and I went out to the tiers to talk to the gang leaders. We needed some kind of a truce between the gangs before we set people free. "We want to let everybody out," Bang told them, "but we can't have people killing each other."

The gang heads agreed and shook hands on it. They would honor a truce for the time being. For now, it was a unifying moment—"us against them."

Before any cells were unlocked, I ran back to my cell and got a blade out from between the cardboard of one of my boxes. Even though I had the gun, I wanted the knife for extra measure. I had my own enemies who would be running loose very soon. Truce or not, I wasn't taking chances. Using a strip of sheeting, I handled it up good and hurried back to the office.

I volunteered to take Officer Davis around to do the unlocking, and the two of us headed out to the tiers. Although the cells on my tier could be unlocked manually, the other tiers were controlled by a lockbox that I did not know how to operate. We started with the tier that housed the most vicious Aryan Warriors. Davis disengaged the locks with a master switch, and the gates opened at once. The Warriors stepped out onto the tier.

We climbed to the second floor, unlocking the gates on death row. I asked my pal, Claude Theriault, if he wanted out. He said no, as he had action on his appeal, which was also the attitude of everyone else on the row. "Frank, watch your back," he told me.

Next was the other upper tier, home to the BMF's most violent players. This is where things got dangerous for me. Before we unlocked their gates, I had Davis walk with me, and I peered into the cells. I could see who was who, including the guy who had stabbed me in the neck with the pen barrel. He and I eyed each other but said nothing. I felt for the gun in my waistband before I nodded for Davis to pull the switch to let them out.

Back downstairs, I told Bang that, except for death row, everybody was out and holding their own. "Okay," he said. "Then unlock the tier gates."

As I unlocked the first one, I saw a sudden movement to my right. It was outside the window on the roof of the chow hall. Snipers! I yelled for everyone to put blankets up on their windows. In short order, all the windows were covered.

As I unlocked the gates, everyone was filing out calmly, as they had promised. But before I unlocked the final tier, home to my enemies, I went to the mop room and adjusted the gun so I could pull it out easily. If I had to, I would use every one of those five .38 shells. I returned to their tier and unlocked it, enabling my enemies to freely wander about. Aside from some hard stares, they steered clear of me, and I of them.

Everyone did their part to keep the windows covered, and a few of the convicts reinforced the main max housing entryway gates, wrapping over a dozen belly chains around the bars, adding restraint cuffs to lock the chains tight, and finishing them off with over a dozen padlocks. We were well barricaded. After that, it was like things should be. People were getting along, catching up, drinking coffee, smoking cigarettes, playing cards, and having fun as though nothing much was going on.

But within myself, I was struggling to hold it together. The gravity of the situation—the fact that any chance of escaping was gone, that Bang-Bang was making it up as he went, that people were having a neighborhood get-together, and that prison guards were being held hostage at gunpoint—overwhelmed me. I felt such an intense rage about the failed plan and the hopeless mess we were now in. I felt for the gun and started for the sergeant's office with an urge to shoot the guards, shoot Bang-Bang for getting us into this, and call Captain Blake and tell him what I'd done.

But as I approached the sergeant's office, I saw an inner door close, which snapped me out of it. I yelled for Bang-Bang, who told me everything was okay, that someone had come through the door to deliver syringes and Demerol.

"Don't worry," he said, "I'll leave a little for you and Incel."

"I don't want any," I told him in disgust. "You're stupid for fogging up your brain when you need it clear."

He batted his hand at me. "It's fine, it's fine," he insisted.

I gave all three guards a Styrofoam cup of coffee, poured one for myself, and listened to Bang's updates. "I just hung up with Blake," he said. "SWAT teams from Carson City and possibly Reno are moving in."

I looked at Incel, who took it in as though he was listening to the weather report. I wanted to wipe the ever-present smile from his face. Then Bang said that Superintendents John Slansky and John Ignacio wanted to negotiate the hostage situation peacefully.

Once again, I felt close to exploding. I had no desire to negotiate with anyone, especially Slansky and Ignacio. I had no use for either one of them. I left Bang and Incel in the office and went back to my cell, where I peeked out the blanket-covered window. It was dark outside. How many hours had passed since Bang-Bang had shown up at my cell, our escape plan in ruins, I could not say. Time held no meaning. All I could see was that it was dark.

I sat on my bunk and thought of my mother, my one true gift in my miserable life. I got a stamped envelope, some writing paper, and a pen. I suddenly felt compelled to tell her how sorry I was for the suffering I had caused her, and that my life's woes were not because she didn't love me enough or had in any way failed me. The words just spilled out. "This isn't your fault," I wrote. "I somehow got lost. Please forgive me for hurting you." Then I begged her for one favor, "Please don't let them bury me in a casket in the ground, for that would be putting me into another cell for eternity."

After I placed the letter in the outbox, I headed back to death row for a final word with Claude Theriault. But when I got to the stairs, I heard a voice yell, "Frank, stop that dude, don't let him get away!" I saw a good-sized inmate round a corner, running as fast as he could with several convicts chasing him with clubs and knives, yelling, "Lying snitch!" I'd never seen him before, but I did nothing to stop him as he flew down the concrete steps only to tumble and fall all the way down. He was covered in blood from head to toe. He'd been beaten, stabbed, and even had some fingers chopped off, with a couple more dangling. Before they could finish him off, Bang-Bang opened the sergeant's office door, gun drawn. He told them to stop or get shot. They stopped.

"Rats aren't part of any truce agreements!" one con said.

Bang pulled the bloodied guy into the office.

I continued to Claude's cell, where we bade each other good-bye. With SWAT teams closing in, I expected that a lot of us would soon die, including me. "Hey, Frank," Claude said with resignation, "it's a fuckin' bitch, but what are you gonna do?"

I went back down to the sergeant's office just as Superintendent Slansky was leaving the office. He saw me but said nothing. My blood pressure shot up. Bang-Bang let me in and told me that he and Slansky had started negotiating. I got mad and told him the Demerol had fucked up his brain as Slansky now knew where everyone was and that this is exactly where they would come when they stormed us. I told him we all had to move, pronto. We hurried the hostages to a cell on a lower tier. Things were getting a little tense between Bang-Bang and me, and he asked me to give back the gun. I kept my word and handed it to him.

With just the knife on me, I started back for my cell when I heard a commotion. "Here they come, here they come!"

I saw the outer door to the mop room burst open, and a bunch of cops carrying M16s and shotguns rushed in. Everyone ran for their cells. I made it to mine where I could see that the entry gates were now wide open. I was amazed. There were no explosions or the sound of saws, yet the SWAT team had busted through the gates that, just hours earlier, had been heavily reinforced with chains and padlocks. There were seven or eight of them dressed in black, and all were armed with fully automatic M16 machine guns, 12-gauge shotguns, and 9-millimeter semi-automatic pistols. It was at that moment that I understood that neither I nor any convict in here, either singly or collectively, stood a chance. We would soon be at their mercy, and not for a minute did I think mercy would be forthcoming.

I was so angry. It was all for nothing. Helplessness is an ugly feeling, and I wished I still had that .38. The thought of dying like some scared coward backed up against a wall in a jail cell filled me with shame. If I had the gun, I could at least restore some dignity by running, yelling, and firing shots in some final act of defiance. That is how I wanted to be remembered.

My reverie was interrupted when a SWAT lieutenant spoke, slowly and distinctly, "You all have exactly sixty seconds to give up and come out, or we will go from cell to cell and kill everything in it."

A moment later, I heard one of the cons call out, "Hey, Bang, show them we mean business and bust a cap!" A second later, the sharp sound of a small-but-loud-caliber bullet let me know Bang had fired.

The SWAT team reacted instantly; the sound of machine-gun fire ripped through the tier with intensity. Twelve-gauge shotguns firing in unison sounded like grenades exploding, while the deep bark of semiautomatic weapons joined in a cacophony of sounds. The deafening release of so much ammo lasted for about twenty seconds, but it felt like forever. Sparks flew as bullets hit steel and ricocheted off. Bullets tore into the concrete walls and ceilings. The bullets that punctured the ceiling blew apart water pipes, causing a stream of water to pour from overhead, flooding the tier. For a few long moments, the only sound was the water spraying from above and splashing on the floor. The smell of cordite was pervasive, and smoke from the firearms wafted all the way down to my cell, the last one on the tier.

Then, the SWAT lieutenant spoke again, "Last time. If I don't hear what I need to hear, I'll give the order."

Someone's voice yelled back, "Hey, not all of us are trying to get killed—some of us want out."

The lieutenant said he would give instructions to each cell and its occupants, and those instructions would be followed, as the repercussions for not obeying commands would be severe. There was a short lull, and then I heard a deep voice ask, "Is there a Frank De Palma somewhere on this tier? If so, speak up."

I didn't know what to think, as I was the only person he inquired about. I stayed silent.

"He's at the end of the tier!" someone called out.

"Frank De Palma!" he repeated.

This time I said, "That's me."

"Are you willing to come out and surrender yourself?"

I wasn't really being given a choice. It was more like "surrender or we'll kill you."

"I'll come out," I said.

"You are to adhere to my orders to the letter. Do you understand?"

I told him I did.

"Clasp your hands behind your head, back up slowly from the cell, and keep walking backwards down the tier. Keep your hands behind your head."

I followed his commands. With every step I took, I thought I was going to be shot. I almost blew it as the water coming down from the ceiling was ice-cold. I made it down to the end of the tier, where I was grabbed and roughed up against the wall, which gave me a bloody nose. I felt the barrel of a shotgun press against the back of my heart, and a SWAT officer leaned down into my ear and spoke in barely a whisper, "Go ahead, say one fucking word."

I couldn't resist. "Like what?"

"You motherfucker!"

I felt a hard blow to the base of my skull, just behind my right ear, and a white light flashed. I felt my clothes being torn from my body and heard the clanking of handcuffs and leg irons locking in place. With my hands cuffed behind my back, I was jerked off the ground and dragged from the max unit, through the door, and yanked outside. Completely naked, cuffed, and shackled, I was shoved to the ground in the cold early morning hours. As I lay on my stomach there, alone, my head throbbing with pain, snow flurries danced in the air.

As time ticked by, other prisoners were walked out, naked,

cuffed, and shackled like I was, and were laid next to one another so each man's face was just inches from the next man's ass. When a few prisoners attempted to create a little space between one another in order to maintain a semblance of dignity, a few of the guards became heavy-handed. My head was throbbing fiercely, my nose felt like a balloon inflating, and it was very cold. It would've been futile to complain or try to reason with the guards. Tensions were high, and adrenaline was flowing. The next twenty-four to seventy-two hours were going to be miserable for us prisoners. What happened from there, I would rather not say.

In the days and weeks that followed, max housing was placed on lockdown. It would be months before we were permitted to leave our cells. But prison officials' main focus was on Bang-Bang, who faced a slew of charges, among them an escape attempt, kidnapping, gun possession, and discharging a firearm. His girlfriend, Teree Lee, was also arrested for smuggling in the guns. But it was not a complete loss, as Bang-Bang managed to successfully negotiate a visit with Teree Lee and was ultimately acquitted of the charges.

Miraculously, neither Incel nor I faced charges. But my fantasies of an idyllic seaside life felt like a cruel joke, leaving me with little more than a sickening memory of myself lying on the ground, shackled and naked, in total defeat.

Some weeks later, in a phone call with my mother, which was facilitated by her sister, who signed my words to her, I assured her that I was fine. She had received that letter I'd sent, which I'd almost forgotten about. "Frankie, Frankie," she cried. She was frantic about my wishes for my burial.

Had I not believed I was going to die that day, I never would have sent it. As I tried to calm her down, I was reminded that despite my lowly prisoner status, someone in this world still loved me.

CHAPTER 15

Silent Night

After the momentary max housing takeover, the next year passed by uneventfully, save for my ongoing war with the BMF, which was now a way of life. Despite several more knife fights, miraculously, no one had died. As the months trudged on, any hopes for parole had been further doused by the additional charge I incurred at the Northern Nevada Correctional Center when I had stabbed Officer Kelly with the spoon handle. Someday, maybe someday, I would get out of here. But I gave it little thought. Staying alive remained front and center.

With the forced medications fully drained from my system, I was once again myself. But what was "myself"? Who was I now? I certainly was no longer the teenager who had naively believed he could do two years in this place and go home. Over the six years of my incarceration, I had adapted to the misery of prison life out of necessity, and in the process, I had changed. I had hardened.

Yet despite this hardening, I still retained elements of my old self, something I discovered when an issue over commissary placed me in a dilemma. The prison commissary was like the corner store, except this one was behind gun towers and barbed wire. Bags of chips, a few varieties of cookies, and plastic-wrapped chocolate treats were a welcome relief from the glop that was ladled out in the culinary. But for me, this was not a pleasure I could enjoy, for the simple reason that I had no money. Whenever my family asked if I needed anything, I told them that no, I was fine. I had disgraced them just by being here, and I did not feel comfortable asking for a thing. But I have to admit to being envious of others when I watched them fill out commissary slips, checking off the things they wanted. Once a week, guards delivered brown bags of the requested items to their cell gates.

My next-door neighbor, a guy named Buck, a regular recipient of overflowing paper bags, noticed that nothing ever came my way. "You want to know where I get the money?" he asked, with a sly smile. "It's simple. I write letters to women and get them to send me a few bucks. I can give you a couple of names if you want."

I immediately did not like the idea of conning lonely women and told him so.

"Suit yourself," he scoffed.

But after a while, the thought of my own paper bag, filled with treats that I hadn't tasted in years, overwhelmed my high moral ground, and I told Buck I'd give it a try.

He gave me two names—Cheryl and Patty. "Now," he said, "what you do is hook them in with a good sob story. Get a nice rapport going, and then you ask for a little money."

As much as I still didn't like the idea, I sat in my cell at night, pen in hand, and created this whole fiction that I was in prison for murder (unjustly, of course) and was sitting on death row. Satisfied with my handiwork, I mailed off the letters and waited. A couple of weeks later, I was excited when they both responded. I started corresponding with the two of them, and although things petered out with Cheryl, Patty and I were hitting it off. She was a single mom with two young children, and I enjoyed receiving her letters and learning about her job and the kids. The only problem was that the more I looked forward to her letters, the worse I began to feel about this whole ruse.

When I reached what felt like the right moment to ask for the money, I stalled.

Buck waved his hand at me in disgust. "What are you waiting for?"

But I just couldn't do it. She was a single mother with very little money herself. At the very moment I should have been most excited, I did not feel like the tough guy I'd become. I felt like a heel. After agonizing over it, I finally decided it just wasn't worth it. I could do without these treats. Once again, I sat on my bunk and penned a carefully worded letter—a letter of confession:

Dear Patty,

You're not going to want anything to do with me after you read this letter. I'm afraid I have been deceiving you. I am not in prison for murder, and I am not on death row. The truth is that my intention in writing to you has been solely to get you to send me money. You're a very nice person, and I'm sorry I've led you on like this. I'm ashamed of myself. I wouldn't blame you for never writing to me again, but I will say that it's been nice to know you.

Yours truly,
Frank

I sealed it up and lay down to sleep, greatly relieved.

A couple of weeks later, I heard back from her. I dreaded opening the envelope, taking a moment to prepare myself for her anger and disgust. I had it coming. But as I read her words, they were not words of rebuke. Quite the opposite. She told me she was so moved by my honesty that she couldn't imagine cutting me loose! I almost laughed out loud. Furthermore, she put a little money into my commissary account. I never expected such a happy outcome. I was excited about the commissary, of course, but what really mattered to me was that I'd made things right with her.

With a clear conscience, I filled out my first commissary request slip. Finally, the brown bag was coming my way. But when I sat down to enjoy my treats, nothing tasted the way I had imagined it. I didn't taste the sweet, just the sour of what I had resorted to. Patty and I wrote back and forth for a while longer till she told me she was getting back with an old boyfriend. I wished her the best.

Ending things with Patty was just as well. Hearing about her job and her family brought me to an outside world I was trying to forget about. The separation from my own family was agony, and I did my best to block out all thoughts of them. But, of course, lying in my cot at night, the thoughts and memories crept in anyway. I was in somewhat regular touch with my dad, who continued to coach me in combat strategies. But it was my mother and sister I thought about most. I thought of Marie and my nephews, who were just babies when I got locked up. I calculated how old they were by now, pained by the thought that I wasn't a part of their young lives and that I was deprived of hearing the word "uncle." I wonder if they even knew about me, the black sheep of the family. Marie and I had spoken a few times by phone in the first couple of years that I was away, but our connection had faded. She was busy with her family, as it should be.

As for my mom, I wrote to her intermittently, always trying to shield her from the ugliness of my life. That letter I had sent her during the max housing takeover was the only lapse—her only glimpse into my reality. I could not let it happen again. And, of course, I couldn't help but wonder what would have happened with me and Vivien. Would we have gotten married? We were only teenagers when we'd met, but still, our love felt like the real thing. Would I have gone back to school and embarked on a serious job path, and would the two of us have started our own family? I struggled hard to blot it out; the thought of what might have been cut deeper than the sharpest blade at the Nevada State Prison.

Family separation was especially hard at the holidays. Though Christmas was just another day at the prison, when it approached, family memories were deeply stirred. One Christmas Eve, late at night, I was lying in my bunk, recalling another Christmas Eve years earlier when I was out with my dad and Wanda, doing some last-minute shopping. I was sitting in the backseat of the car, staring out the window, when I mindlessly began singing, "Chestnuts Roasting on an open fire, Jack Frost nipping at your nose . . ."

Wanda turned around, a look of amazement on her face.

I caught Dad looking back at me in the rearview mirror. "Hey," he said, "you've got a good voice."

"Where did you get that voice?" Wanda asked.

Feeling embarrassed, I stopped.

"No, keep singing!" they both cried. "Keep singing!"

My heart warmed at the memory of my dad smiling at me that day, delighted by my previously unknown talent—looking at me with pride. I always wanted him to be proud of me.

Lying there on my bunk, recalling that day, I started humming, and once again mindlessly drifted into song. "Chestnuts Roasting on an open fire, Jack Frost nipping at your nose . . . Yuletide . . ." Then I stopped and just lay there, remembering.

From down the tier came a voice, "Keep singing!"

I was startled. I didn't know I'd been overheard.

Another voice called out, "Sing!"

And so I did. I sang any Christmas carol I could think of. I didn't know all the words to any of them, so I patched them together as best I could.

Dashing through the snow, in a one-horse open sleigh, all the . . . . Hey!

Jingle bells, jingle bells . . . .

I'm dreaming of a White Christmas . . . may your days be merry and bright . . . .

Silent, holy night . . . sleep in heavenly peace, sleep in heavenly peace . . .

Every time I stopped, my tier mates clamored for more, so I kept going, pulling faded carols from old memories. When there were no songs left and no voice left in me, I fell quiet, as did the rest of the tier.

CHAPTER 16

A Deadly Confrontation

Saturday morning, May 15, 1982, is a date I will never forget. I was a couple of weeks shy of my twenty-sixth birthday, and I was playing cards with a guy named Roderick Abeyta. I knew him about as well as I knew anybody else, which is to say, not well at all. Just another morning, another card game to try to pass the time.

Abeyta was inside his cell, dealing cards from a cardboard box that served as a table. I was on the tier-side, sitting on a plastic five-gallon bucket, reaching through the bars to play. But I wasn't focused on the game. I was unsettled for some reason. Abeyta looked at me and shrugged, as if to say, "What's the problem?"

Something just didn't feel right, and I wished I had my knife with me. Ever since the Danny Jackson murder and the tighter security measures that had been implemented, pat-down searches were common. I had to be careful to avoid carrying a knife all the time. But I was starting to regret having left it back in my cell.

And then I heard the whisper—*Frank*—and everything went into slow motion. I caught sight of something shiny in my peripheral vision and pulled back just as it came for me, missing my neck but slashing my shoulder. I was on my feet. Abeyta tossed me a shank; I caught it and clenched it tight as my attacker came at me again. I swung at him wildly, ducking his knife and shoving mine into him, adrenaline gushing through me. He kept coming until he went down. I'd stabbed him four times.

As he lay on the floor, I dropped the knife and stood over him, my body shaking. "Why, man? Why?"

He looked up at me through half-closed eyelids and whispered, "They told me to get you." Then he looked past me and started to smile, like he recognized someone.

Guards and medics arrived, and I was told to go back to my cell, where I sat still on my bunk.

A little while later, a sergeant came by, and I asked him how the guy was doing. "He's dead."

I hung my head.

They took me to the infirmary where they stitched my shoulder. After that, I was moved from my cell in max housing to what was known as the "last-night cell"—the cell where the condemned spend the night before they are put to death. The message was not lost on me.

In the days that followed, I was sick at heart. It's no small thing to take a person's life. I learned his name was Glen Stewart and that he had been prospecting for the BMF. He'd been dispatched to kill me and almost had, his barber's razor just missing my jugular. My emotions vacillated from fear to remorse to anger. Mostly anger. Anger that people are put into a hellhole like this and forced to fight for their lives—every single day. Anger that their best hope is joining a gang. Glen Stewart was just another con trying to survive, trying to "make his bones" for the BMF. I could only imagine what they had told their young prospect: "Hey, brother, you up to it? I love you, brother. Go on now, get him—go out there and make your bones. You can do it."

Now he was dead, and I sat alone in the last-night cell, a barred gate separating me from the gas chamber. The chamber door was open, and I could see two chairs. Under each one was a porcelain tub that held hydrochloric acid. There was a pulley above each chair with chains that served to lower a sack of cyanide eggs into the tubs, thus releasing the cyanide gas. Sooner or later, I might very well be strapped into one of those chairs. I stared at the chairs, asking myself, *Will they try to execute me for this? If I am sentenced to die, will I die like a coward? Will I fall apart in front of a bunch of giddy reporters detailing my hysteria to the world?* I imagined myself choking on the deadly fumes.

I forced myself to get up and face what might likely be my fate. The barred gate was unlocked, and I slid it open and stepped into the deadly chamber. Slowly, I lowered myself into one of the chairs, my entire body shaking. I played out what I imagined a death like this—of poison and suffocation—would feel like. It was so real. Panicked as I felt, my body started finding calmness, and I just sat there for a while before getting up and walking back to the cell. The exercise of exposing myself to such an ending helped me to see that, if the time came, I'd hold my mud. I would not make a spectacle of myself.

Glen Stewart's death made it to the newspapers. At first, it was reported as a gang-related contract killing. I guess they changed their minds as the next headline said I'd killed him because he'd found out I was making a homemade gun and he had snitched to the authorities. Another story maintained that it was a racially motivated killing. None of it was true. Yes, Glen Stewart was Black, but I hadn't noticed the color of his skin when it went down. The only thing I'd noticed was the razor he was brandishing when he tried to cut my throat.

But much of the media speculation was doused by an article in the *Reno Gazette-Journal* where Warden George Sumner said he doubted there was any gang contract on Stewart's life. He said, "De Palma killed him on his own, as far as I'm concerned. I don't think there was any big conspiracy." Then he added, "De Palma was a hate-filled Nazi type."

Sumner was closest to the truth. There was no conspiracy, and I was never any Nazi, but hate-filled? Absolutely! I'd been sent to this place on a "nickel and dime" charge, and I was paying for it with my entire life. Damn right I was angry!

They kept me in that last-night cell for several months before I was moved back to max housing where I would await my trial, which would be a good year away. I already knew my plea: not guilty by reason of self-defense.

As my life hung in the balance, I resumed my daily routine as best I could. Get up, go out to the yard, work out, eat, and wish I'd never seen the inside of this hell on earth. I had plenty of time to think about what had happened and how my own path was steadily worsening. After the Stewart killing, the other convicts treated me much differently. In prison, as always, the more violent you are, the greater the esteem, and I had garnered great respect. But at what price?

Not a day went by that I didn't think of Glen Stewart and wish it had never happened. And every day I prayed the truth would come out at the trial and that the jury would see that I had killed him in self-defense. I felt fortunate that I had two eyewitnesses—a porter who was swabbing the floor on the opposite tier and, of course, Rod Abeyta, who'd tossed me the shank. I actually hadn't seen Abeyta since that fateful morning. He'd mysteriously disappeared, which made me a little uneasy.

As I dwelled on the trial, I was not only sick at heart, but I also wasn't feeling very well. I was so tired, and at twenty-six-years-old, I had little energy. I went to the infirmary where the doctor drew blood. A week later, I learned that I'd tested positive for hepatitis C. The doctor explained that it's often spread through dirty needles, and he checked my arms for track marks. There weren't any. "Get high and die" was still my mantra. But my tattoos were the giveaway. When he'd asked how I'd gotten them, I told him how I'd injected the ink using a straightened paper clip that I'd sharpened on the cell floor, never giving a thought to germs or sanitary hazards. I'd picked it up from dirty paper clips, and now hepatitis was running rampant in my body.

He suggested treatment with a drug called interferon. He said it had a 50 percent cure rate and that, without any intervention, the disease and ensuing liver complications could prove fatal. This was very serious. To get started, I would need a liver biopsy, which he told me was risky. After he laid it all out, I didn't think about it long. I declined the treatment. I figured I'd be dead soon anyway, either killed by the BMF or by the State of Nevada. Why bother?

Fortunately, my energy level inexplicably rebounded. Once again, I felt fine, although I knew the damage to my liver was quietly progressing. I didn't care.

My first lawyer was a public defender named Todd Reese, whom I quickly dubbed the "public pretender." My only contact with this guy was over the phone. He never once came out to the prison to meet me in person and review the case. I understood that public defenders carry impossible caseloads, but a case like mine was as serious as it got. The first time we spoke, he told me he was pretty sure he could get the death penalty off the table in exchange for "life without"—meaning, life without parole.

Life without parole was another death sentence. I felt a flash of anger and lashed out at him. "How come you aren't up here talking to me in person—running that past me to my face? Yes, I killed the guy. But I didn't murder him. I did not murder Glen Stewart. I defended myself. You're fired!"

Reese had himself removed from the case. My next lawyer was a woman who came out to the visit house but was too timid to sit down and talk to me. She quickly vanished, making room for a man named Martin Wiener, my new court-appointed private counsel. Unlike the public pretender and the timid lady,

Mr. Wiener came out to the prison, sat right down with me, and paid attention to every detail as I laid out what had happened. He believed me. I told him I wanted to plead not guilty by reason of self-defense. With that, we prepared for trial.

With my life hinging on the trial outcome, it was a tense wait, with almost a year of cycles and surges of emotions that ranged from soaring hopes for exoneration to plunging despair at the prospect of execution or worse—spending the rest of my life locked away in prison. Some days I felt like I was going crazy. I tried to distract myself however I could, often seeking solace in the wildlife that made their home inside the prison walls.

They didn't come close to Bud, but I still enjoyed the feral cats that freely came and went, often wandering into our cells. My regular visitor was a dirty brown cat. I was always happy to see her. I didn't have a name for her or anything like that, as naming her would mean an attachment. I always offered her a little food and milk, which she happily ate and lapped up. One day, she trotted into my cell and jumped up on my bunk. As she did, all this brown liquid shot out of her, spreading all over my blanket.

"Hey man, what's wrong?" I looked closer and saw she was starting to deliver kittens. Before I realized what was happening, two newborns lay next to her, and I could see that another one was coming. But then the mama started crying in a strange way, and I knew something wasn't right. I leaned in closer to see a tiny paw and leg coming out of her. The kitten was coming out upside down, and it was stuck. The mother's cries were getting louder. I had no idea what to do, so instinctively, I reached in and found the other leg. Holding the two legs together, I gently tugged, and lo and behold, the little kitten was born. I'd done it! As I laid the tiny kitten next to its mother, the whole world around me seemed to disappear—the trial, Glen Stewart, the

BMF, everything. In a moment of pure joy, the heavy weight and ugliness of it all was gone. Two more kittens followed, and I stood back with pride as the mother licked and nursed her litter. These were my kittens!

For a couple of weeks, I happily watched over mother and brood in a box that somebody gave me. Guards stopped by my cell and warned me the cats had to go. But what to do with them? When kittens were born inside here, most of the cons simply broke their necks and flushed them down the toilet. There was no way I could do anything like that. I sought out one of the more decent guards and asked for his help, and he agreed to take them to a no-kill shelter.

When the time came, I walked my box of kittens through the tiers, getting laughed at by the other convicts. But I didn't care. I bade goodbye to each one of them and handed the box to the guard. I wasn't convinced he had any intention of taking them to the shelter, but that's what he'd promised me. I hoped he would keep his promise.

CHAPTER 17

A Jury of One's Peers

In June 1983, a little over a year after I'd killed Glen Stewart, my trial began at the Carson City Courthouse. I sat in a suit and tie my father had bought for me, listening as the charges against me were read off: first-degree capital murder, second-degree murder, and manslaughter. If I was found guilty of the top charge, the district attorney would seek the death penalty.

My dad came to the courthouse for most of the trial. It was nice to see him, a very different man from the father I had grown up with. He and Wanda had divorced, and he was now married to his third wife. It was in the aftermath of my having killed Glen Stewart that he had found Jesus. I guess having your son, who maybe you loved after all, facing execution by the state was enough for any parent to do some serious thinking.

The prosecutor was a woman named Brooke Nielsen, and it was clear that she was on a mission to see me put to death. In her opening statements, she portrayed me as a monster who set out to deliberately and viciously kill Glen Stewart.

In turn, my attorney Mr. Wiener portrayed the killing as a matter of self-defense. Quite simply, if I had not killed Glen Stewart, Glen Stewart would have killed me.

Miss Nielsen started off by calling her star witness to the stand. Out stepped Roderick Abeyta. Since he'd disappeared from the prison shortly after that fateful morning, I'd begun to suspect he was being kept under wraps for this very moment. But I couldn't imagine what he would say that would work for the prosecution.

Under oath, Abeyta said the killing was not spontaneous, that it had been planned. Furthermore, he said I had forced him to sharpen the knife and then hand it over.

"And what if you didn't agree to do what he wanted?" Miss Nielsen asked.

Avoiding any eye contact with me, Abeyta replied, "He said if I didn't do it, he'd come into my cell, cut my heart out, and show me what a heart looks like."

I was on my feet. *"What?!"*

The judge banged his gavel and told me to sit down.

"But this is ridiculous! Nothing was planned. This is a big lie."

"Sit down, Mr. De Palma—sit down!" the judge barked. With that, he ordered a recess to have a word with me.

He told me there were to be no more outbursts. If I did it again, I would be removed from the courtroom and the trial would continue without me. He told me to think about it for a few minutes, which I did. I didn't know how I was supposed to just sit there and listen to these lies. My life was on the line. But I had no choice other than to assure the judge I would abide by his orders. There was no way I could not be present at my own trial. I would remain silent as my heart sank.

As Abeyta continued with this ridiculous work of fiction, he steadfastly avoided any eye contact with me. I stared him down throughout, starting to get the picture. Rod Abeyta was likely slated to spend the rest of his life in the hellhole known as the Nevada State Prison. This trial was his ticket out. Testifying in a capital case like this was a once-in-a-lifetime opportunity. Not only was he holding the winning lottery ticket—he had the power ball. He would parrot anything they fed him. Part of me couldn't blame him.

On cross-examination, my lawyer asked Abeyta about his incentives in testifying against me, and as Abeyta stumbled through the questions, his credibility was shredded. But it hardly mattered; the trial was never going to be about the truth.

Next up for the prosecution was a replay of my attack on Officer Kelly at the Northern Nevada Correctional Center two years earlier, when I had been subjected to the forced Prolixin injections. My lawyer objected, maintaining that this was a separate incident with no bearing on the case at hand. But the judge overruled it. My lawyer called an expert witness to the stand, a psychiatrist named Dr. John Chappel, who testified as to my desperate and altered mindset when that assault took place. Dr. Chappel said that the forced injections were tantamount to chemical lobotomy and chemical torture. Hearing it in those terms was the first time I fully comprehended the enormity of what had been done to me by Robert Francis Freeman. I just hoped the jury would see my attack on Officer Kelly within that context.

On my behalf, my lawyer called Chris Jones, the porter who'd witnessed everything from the opposite tier as he'd swabbed the floor. His testimony was the one pure moment in a courthouse of lies. Cynically, I wondered how the prosecution had failed to broker a cheap deal with him, too. For his efforts, he'd been held outside in a hot van for four hours instead of being afforded the comfort of the air-conditioned courthouse while he waited to testify. When he was finally brought in from outside, he was sweat-soaked and angry but still managed to pull himself together and tell the truth.

Miss Nielsen's next move was to inflame the passions of the jury by bringing in a parade of guards to testify as to what a louse I was. Their character assassinations were not germane to the case. But it didn't matter to a jury who hung on to every one of their words.

They say you're judged by a jury of your peers. I looked at these twelve people who were to decide my fate, people who had no idea about the desperation inside a maximum-security prison, a world unto itself, one that could never be compared with the real world. These were not my peers. If this was truly to be a jury of my peers, then the jury box would have been filled with prisoners, gangbangers, Aryan Warriors, and anyone else unfortunate enough to dwell within the walls of the Nevada State Prison. Those were my peers, and it was they who could have accurately judged me. Of course, that was a fantasy. I was to be judged by everyday people—housewives, mailmen, secretaries—who believed the noble inscriptions on courthouse walls, who believed that prisons are humane and that the word of law enforcement is the word of God. How could they understand that I lived in a place where violence was normalized? I would like to have asked them to step in my shoes and tell me exactly what they would have done differently. I would like to have told them a thing or two about these shiny, upstanding guards who were testifying against me. But, of course, it was nothing more than wishful thinking. I sat in silence.

After about ten days, both sides rested. But before the judge gave the jurors their instructions, I requested a word with him. During the trial, I'd reached a decision within myself, and I spoke from my heart. "Your honor, this lady has done nothing but try to portray me as some fire-breathing monster, which is not who I am. It's been very hard for me to sit quietly and listen to all of this. I have one request. Can you please ask the jury to either find me guilty of capital murder, or acquit me? I don't want any in-between. I don't want lesser verdicts. I don't want a conscience verdict—something they can live with. It's either guilty, and I'll be executed, or not guilty by reason of self-defense. All or nothing, your honor. Please."

The judge listened, but shook his head no. "I admire your convictions, Mr. De Palma, but by law, I have to give instructions that these lesser charges be considered."

After a day of deliberating, the jury was ready. I looked at my dad and then Mr. Wiener, and I stood up for the verdict. Just as I expected, they opted for the middle ground—second-degree murder. The sentence was five years to life. There was the possibility of parole, but I knew it wouldn't be in any five years, ten years, twenty years—if ever.

My life was over.

CHAPTER 18

The Dark Years

With the loss of my murder trial and what amounted to a life sentence, all hope left me. I could feel it leave, like the spirit leaving the body. At the age of twenty-seven, my hopes, my dreams were all over. I would never regain a normal life. I would never love a woman, become a father, have a family of my own. I would never find a career and live out a natural, normal existence. Instead, I would be relegated to this soulless place for what might be the rest of my life.

I struggled to somehow come to terms with it, but the enormity of it was unbearable. What had I done to deserve this? I did not murder Glen Stewart; I killed him in self-defense. If I hadn't killed him, he would have killed me. As I crumbled to pieces inside, my anger grew at the unfairness of it all. It was an anger toward a justice system that I had naively believed was about truth. It was an anger at the farce of a "correctional" institution that functioned as anything but. But most of all, I was angry at God. *Why is all of this happening to me? What have I ever done to deserve this?*

There were no answers, of course, but where there had once been a sliver of hope, all light was extinguished, replaced by an inferno of rage. If this was the life I was meant for, then I would go beyond adapting to it—I would embrace it. All the hatred and darkness of the Nevada State Prison would manifest in me. I felt like my life had been stolen from me, and now I would take my pound of flesh.

Fueled by rage, I prepared to do battle like never before. I paced my cell, strategizing. The BMF would never get me; *I* would get *them*. They were responsible for my not getting parole after my first two years, for sending their gangbangers to rape me, for turning my life into a perpetual knife fight. I would get every single one of them, and I would devote my every waking moment to that goal.

Out in the yard, I pushed harder at the weights. If anyone lifted more than I did, then I saw him as a threat and had no peace till I lifted as much or more. I worked my way up to benching four hundred pounds. I was a maniac at the weight pile. My biceps were huge, and I had to cut open the inseam in my pants to accommodate my bulging quads. I decided my tattoos needed to look even scarier, and the scariest thing I could think of was the image of a swastika. I sharpened another paperclip and inked in the evil symbol on one of my biceps. Hepatitis be damned!

A lone warrior, I became a fearsome sight, and most steered clear of me. I spoke to no one. I devolved into a primitive, primordial being, accessing my most basic amygdala level. It was about survival and nothing else. The blind spots I had always taken care to avoid? Now I owned them. This is where I dwelled, and this is where I struck. I kept my shanks sharpened and my focus sharper, always listening for that whisper . . .

Frank . . .

The slashes on my wall kept notching up. Everyone was my enemy now.

When two notorious sex offenders hit the yard, I almost killed one of them when he had the nerve to saunter up to me and say, "Hi, Frank." I somehow refrained from stabbing him on the spot. "You ever speak to me again," I seethed, "I will end you." And I would have. But others took care of it. The two of them were quickly stabbed up and killed. Good riddance.

But nothing got my blood boiling like the unexpected sight of Dr. Robert Francis Freeman, the criminal doctor from the Northern Nevada Correctional Center. I was coming in from the yard one afternoon and there he was, chatting with somebody in the hall. As soon as he saw me, his face lit up, all friendly. "Hey, Frank, how ya doing?"

Though I was shackled and cuffed, I rushed him, hoping to body slam him, sink my teeth into his neck if I could, and, with a little luck, hit his jugular. But the guards pulled me back before I got close enough. I must have looked like a madman, but I had become a madman. I did not care. At least I got to see the look of fear on his face.

As I became fully immersed in my depraved existence, I forgot about my family, forgot that a whole world existed beyond these walls. This, and this alone, was my world. I dwelled in a black hole of deep darkness. After the trial, I rarely replied to the letters my mom sent me. Although my dad visited me every so often, his visits were not good for me. They were stressful, as they threw me off, taking me to some semblance of normality. It was too much, too confusing, and very difficult for me to get refocused after he was gone. During one visit, he asked me why I was so full of hate. I told him hate was the only thing keeping me alive. He said that if I was to be released from prison, the public would not be safe. I did not disagree with him.

My war with the guards intensified, if that was even possible. They hated me, and I hated them even more. In another brutal encounter with them, I withstood a birdshot assault that should have killed me. Once again, it happened out in the pen when I was slugging it out with a guy from the BMF. The guard in the gun tower fired a warning shot and shouted for the two of us to get on the ground, which neither of us did. He fired a second round, and this time, he ordered us to get on our hands and knees and crawl to the side of the pen. My enemy dropped to the ground. I shouted up at the tower, "Fuck you! I'll get on my hands and knees for no one but my mother!"

Then I grabbed the chain-link fence to brace myself for what I knew was coming. The guard leveled the shotgun at me and unloaded, firing again and again, stopping twice to reload, before blasting me again. I clung to the fence, feeling the impact of the birdshot and the warmth of blood drenching my shirt. He just kept coming. As I was losing consciousness, I heard frantic shouts, "Cease fire! Cease fire!"

I woke up in the hospital, where I learned he'd sprayed me with birdshot eleven times. The use of force was so excessive that I believe he'd intended to kill me. He knew he could get away with it. If I had died, so what? One less convict for them to count. And the doctors said I should have died, but somehow, I didn't. The pellets hit every part of my body, causing nerve damage in my legs. The doctors picked out as much of it as they could, from my head and face down to my toes and even the bottoms of my feet. Eventually, they gave up, advising me that the rest of it would work its way out over time. Some of it did, but most of the pellets are inside me to this day, as is the residual leg numbness.

Lying in that hospital bed, all I thought about was pulverizing that tower guard. For his part, he was suspended for thirty days. When he returned, I wanted to break his neck, and I verbally threatened him in the halls. But I never got to do more than that. He'd made enemies out of too many prisoners and was smart enough to move about cautiously, always in the company of other guards, never alone.

Over the years, I found that there are basically three kinds of guards: the corrupt ones, like those on the Aryan Warrior payroll; the haters, like Lieutenant Harrison, the guy who came to my hospital bedside with a tape recorder after the first knife attack; and the ones just doing their jobs. It was this third category that always gave me pause, even in my darkened state. In particular, I thought of a guard nicknamed Lou. I imagined him going home at night, being greeted by a wife and little children after putting in a day of honest work. There was an inexplicable personal connection between Lou and me. It was as if he recognized the reality of this prison and of my desperate plight within it. Without a word, he would periodically drop off a paper bag at my cell. Inside was contraband that had been confiscated, including steel blanks, which I hid away for sharpening. His actions shocked and baffled me, but the only thing I could surmise was that he was trying to help me. I was deeply moved that at least one human being on this planet—and a guard, at that—understood and cared.

So, when I learned that a plan was afoot to make a deadly move on Lou, I paced my cell. A few gangbangers were going to stab him up for reasons I was not privy to. But I'd gotten enough details to know the threat was real. I wanted to warn him, but to do so was crossing the snitch line. But it was also a bit of a gray area—not exactly ratting. Actually, many of the cons would have supported a decision to tip him off, not because it was the right thing to do but because he would have been indebted to me, which would have given me a chip to play. Chip or not, I kept imagining his children learning their father had been stabbed and possibly killed. As hardened as I had become, I couldn't shake that image.

I decided to tell him. I had to. He took my warning seriously, and when a couple of cons, shanks in hands, were found near Lou's regular post during the night, Lou was nowhere to be found.

Lou never said anything further about it, but I could feel his gratitude when I passed him in the halls. As far as that chip I'd earned, I didn't give it much thought until sometime later when a dire situation called it into play.

My next-door neighbor was a guy named Spike, who was a major heroin user. On the other side of Spike was Pops, also heavy into heroin. This was the same Pops I'd met when I'd first entered the Nevada State Prison some twelve years earlier, the one who'd warned me to "expect the unexpected." Over the years, he'd shared a few more words—not many, but I'd developed a sense of protectiveness for the old guy.

One morning, Spike had gotten in a sizable haul of heroin, which he shared with Pops. That night, Spike was cooking it up in his cooker. I knew Spike was going at it hard. Later on, it got awfully quiet in Spike's cell. I stepped out on the tier and looked in on him. He was lying on the floor, his eyes open, staring, but not moving. It didn't look like he was breathing. I knew I wasn't supposed to do anything—*Let him go, let him be free*. I ran over to Pops's cell to see what he thought. For a second, I thought I detected a flicker of life in those old blue eyes. I was even more surprised when he said, "Frank, do what your heart tells you to do."

I did a double take as this was not prison talk. I looked at Pops like I was seeing him for the first time.

I didn't think I had any heart left, but I must have because I raced down the tier for help, barely hearing Pops calling after me, "And, Frank, I won't be at breakfast in the morning!"

I found Officer Lou and told him Spike had overdosed. Lou radioed for help and the two of us ran back to his cell. The drugs and cooker were on open display, which could be another criminal charge for Spike. I begged Lou to look the other way. He told me to get back in my cell, which I did. Next thing I knew, he was at my bars, passing me the cooker and the drugs. "See that you get rid of it."

There was much drama on the tier as medics worked on Spike before he was placed on a stretcher and taken to the hospital. After everything finally died down, and the tier fell quiet, I fell asleep. But at some point during the night, I sat up, awakened by a loud gasp. Everyone on the tier must have heard it. Suddenly, I remembered Pops's words to me as I'd run for help hours earlier. In the urgency of the moment, I hadn't quite pieced together his intent to overdose. But I knew the gasp was coming from Pops. He was gone. I settled back in my bunk, hoping the man was finally free and at peace.

Next morning, they fished Pops's body out of his cell and dragged it onto the tier, the guards and the coroner laughing it up, talking about using his body as a table to make chicken salad sandwiches. I trembled with anger. "You cock-suckin' motha'fuckers!" I shouted. "He was my friend!"

"Take it easy, De Palma! Take it easy!" the guards yelled back.

But at least the coroner apologized. "No, that wasn't right," he said. "We shouldn't have been so disrespectful. Sorry about that."

A few days later, Spike returned from the hospital. I was unsure how he'd react to me once he learned I was the one who'd summoned help. I didn't know if he'd be angered by my interference, but he smiled when he saw me. "Thank you, Frank. You did the right thing. I'm glad to still be here."

Later that day, we were outside when Spike pulled me to the yard phone and told me to speak to his mother, who lived in Alabama. With her coughing, raspy voice, I got an image of a chain-smoking middle-aged woman hooked up to oxygen. "Thank you, Frank. You saved m'boy's life! That's m'boy! Spike's my number one!"

I told her it was quite all right, and she replied, "It's more than all right! You listen to me, Frank De Palma. You need something—anything—you let me know!"

"Yes, ma'am!"

It was a nice moment. But much of the credit also belonged

to Officer Lou, who took such capable charge of the emergency. He was a good man, and I was grateful he had been there that night.

But my warmth for him was the exception. For the others, I felt cold hatred. For their part, they returned the favor. They hassled me constantly, showing up at my cell in the middle of the night, ordering me out so they could toss my cell for contraband, which included a humiliating strip search and throwing my few possessions all over the place. But I fought back every step of the way. When they showed up and ordered me out, I always refused, meaning they would have to "extract" me. I was never an easy extraction. I was always up for a fight, but being outnumbered by them, it was more like a beating. Somehow, I did not care. My fear was eclipsed by rage. There was more at stake than my physical well-being.

One morning they arrived and ordered me to "cuff up," which meant I should hold out my arms for handcuffs, and they would lead me out of the cell. They'd already awakened me several hours earlier and searched the cell. They knew I had no weapons. They were here simply to hassle me. "Fuck you!" was my response.

I guess that day they were tired of fighting me. Even though they always got me in the end, I still managed to get off a few good ones, and maybe they just weren't in the mood for a punch in the face. But they couldn't just walk away, either. "Okay," they said, smiling, and left—for the moment.

I didn't know what was next, but I was on my feet, ready. A few minutes later they were back, pulling a stretched-out fire hose. They pushed the nozzle through the bars of my cell and aimed it directly at me. I quickly pulled my mattress from my bunk and held it up like a shield, just as the powerful spray of water was unleashed. The force of it pushed me against the wall and I held onto that mattress with everything I had. I managed to hang on for maybe fifteen minutes before the water-logged weight of it became unbearable and my fingers gave way. Then the rush of water came directly at me, pinning me to the wall. They all laughed as I twisted my head this way and that, coughing and choking, trying to draw air into my lungs.

I hated them. I hated all of them. But I don't think my rage was entirely about them. In the end, I was fighting for my soul. It was about the only thing left of me.

CHAPTER 19

Not Meant for Human Consumption

By 1989, the Nevada State Prison was well over one hundred years old, had fallen into disrepair, and was in the process of being shut down. Most of the prison population was to be transferred to the newly built Ely State Prison, located in a desolate region about three hundred miles east of Carson City, close to the Utah border.

It had been fifteen years since I'd been incarcerated, six since I'd lost my murder trial. And during that time, it had been an astonishing thirteen years that I'd been battling the BMF. There were now thirty-seven slashes on my wall. About twenty of them were fights that never actually happened but in which a knife had been shown, so they counted as far as I was concerned. But seventeen slashes represented actual attempts on my life. I recalled each incident clearly, especially, of course, the deadly fight with Glen Stewart. Though I had survived these battles, I could never assume that I would survive a thirty-eighth encounter. But number thirty-eight would never come.

As the transfer to the new prison drew closer, things took a most surprising turn. While I naturally assumed my battles with the BMF would continue at Ely, several Aryan Warriors took me aside and told me they wanted it to end. Pat McKenna's power over the Warriors had waned, and with the respect I'd earned over the years, ranking gang members decided that even though I was not one of their own, they would no longer sit on the sidelines while I was attacked. They would come to my defense. But they also said that their interference with the BMF's agenda for me could trigger a full-blown race war, and neither the Warriors nor the BMF wanted that. Several Black Independents also implored me to end it. They told me the BMF was willing to bury the hatchet.

My answer: "Hell no!" The Black Mafia Family had taken *everything* from me. I had been twenty years old and due to get out in eight months when four of them had tried to rape me. And because I had defended myself, they'd tried to kill me, sending Glen Stewart and scores of others to end my life. As far as I was concerned, this would end when I was dead or every single one of them was laid out cold.

But everyone kept after me, asking me to reconsider, telling me Ely would be a new leaf and that it was time to let it go. "Nobody wants a race war," they all said.

Under pressure from all quarters, I reluctantly agreed to a meeting with the BMF's shot caller, a guy named Duke, along with a corrections lieutenant.

The three of us sat down, Duke and I staring at each other, controlled hatred in our eyes. Were we not sitting in this office, knives would have been flashing. Duke broke the silence, "We're ready to end it."

"And the green light?" I asked.

"It's off. No one from our side will make a move on you again. I wasn't here when everything went down in the beginning, but I run things now, and it's done. You have my word."

"What do you say, De Palma?" the lieutenant asked. "All feuds end at some point."

I fell quiet. Fighting this gang had morphed into a way of life. It was hard to imagine it could ever really end. But it had been a long time, too long, so much hatred, so much blood.

I slowly nodded. "But! If one of your guys even looks at me cockeyed, it's on!"

"They won't," Duke insisted. "We need to end this. There's already been too much blood spilled. No one will make a move on you again. I promise you. I promise you, man." He reached out his hand.

Before I shook it, I told him, "Where I come from, a handshake means something, even more than ink to paper."

"That's what it means where I come from, too."

The two of us stood up and shook. It was over. After so many years of waking up every single day, wondering if this was the day they would get me, it was done. And it was not lost on me that they were coming to me to end it, which gave me a little satisfaction.

When the day came to finally leave the prison for good, I boarded a van in the early morning hours for the six-hour drive to Ely. I was thirty-four years old and had spent nearly half my life at the Nevada State Prison. As the bus rolled off the grounds, I never looked back.

Along the drive, the mood in the van was quiet, reflective. Even though we were destined for another prison, it was someplace new and different; our faces were pressed to the windows as we rolled up to its gates. Though it was a spanking new prison, it was depressing to behold—cold concrete, steel bars, silver razor wire—a grim eyesore on the barren landscape. A refrigerated truck parked out front was unloading our food, the pallets containing cases of food that were stamped in black lettering big enough for us to read: NOT MEANT FOR HUMAN CONSUMPTION.

Life at Ely went on much the same as at the Nevada State Prison. New gangs formed, each one jockeying for power. Bets were taken on how long before somebody got killed. It was actually a few months before a gay guy was fatally stabbed, a little longer than most thought it would take.

A few months after my arrival at Ely, I got wind of a rumor that Roderick Abeyta, the prosecution's star witness against me at my murder trial, was back in prison. His phony-baloney story had bought him his freedom, but now he was back, convicted of capital murder for killing a woman after he'd been released. Though he was housed on death row, I ran into him in the infirmary. I was finishing up a routine appointment when I saw his face in the window of a holding cell. I walked over to his door and stared at him for a hard moment. He averted his eyes, the same way he'd done at the trial.

"So," I said, "you're back, huh? I was your ticket out of here. I paid for your lies. The least you could have done was to have stayed out."

He shrugged. "You don't have to worry about getting me. The state's going to do it for you. I dropped my appeals—fuck it. I'm just waiting on a date. They're going to execute me. I'm going to die in here."

"Good for you," I said, and continued on my way.

Without my war with the BMF, life at Ely somehow felt strange and unfamiliar. Duke had kept his word. Although I remained leery of them, and as they were of me, no one from their gang made a move, and I laid down my weapons as well. Horrible as those years had been, fighting to stay alive also gave me a purpose, and without that purpose, I felt a little lost, a bit confused. But I was adjusting. I was back at the weight bench with my usual enthusiasm, now pressing 460 pounds, which would be my top weight.

I also got a job as a supply clerk, filling requisition orders for prison supplies, which I delivered when they came in. I worked at a desk and sat next to a civilian worker, feeling like a regular Joe. Although I didn't get paid, as most prison jobs were non-paid, it occupied my time, and I rather liked it. But it came to an end when another convict working in the same department got busted for drugs and we were all fired.

My next job was out at the weight piles, which I also enjoyed. There were three separate piles: one for whites, one for Blacks, and the other for Hispanics and any other non-whites. I maintained order on the lines, kept the weights stacked properly, and made sure nobody walked off with any of them. Weightlifting was my passion, so this job was a natural for me.

One afternoon, I was in the infirmary, locked inside a holding cell, waiting to see a doctor, when I heard a lot of commotion out in the clinic. I went to the cell door and looked through the window where I could see the warden holding a bundle of white blankets in his arms. Nurses and guards were coming up to him, smiling and clucking and cooing at what must have been a baby. A must unusual sight in prison.

As he turned to show the baby to all the clinic staff, he noticed me looking on from my window and walked toward my cell. "Unlock this door!" he ordered the nearest guard.

"But De Palma's in there," the guard protested.

"I know who's in there," the warden said. "Now open it!"

After a moment of hesitation, the door was dutifully unlocked and swung open. Standing there was Warden Charles Wolff, holding the tiny bundle. I blinked hard, struggling to make sense of it.

"Hello, Frank."

"Hello, Warden."

"Frank, would you like to hold my new granddaughter?"

It took me a moment, but I nodded. "Yes, I would."

I think the guard who unlocked the door collapsed.

The warden carefully handed me the small bundle, and just like that, I, Frank De Palma, one of the most violent prisoners in the system, was cradling a baby girl in my arms—the warden's granddaughter, no less. I clucked and smiled at her, awed by her delicate beauty. "You know, Warden," I said, "all you have to do is look at a newborn baby to know there's a God."

The warden smiled. Others were gathering around, clamoring for a chance to hold her. "No," he said. "Only Frank."

It was truly one of the highlights of my life.

I had no idea why Warden Wolff would allow someone like me to hold his precious granddaughter. I was confounded by it, puzzling about it for days. The only thing I could conclude was that he knew I would never hurt her, that there was something fundamentally decent about me. He must have seen some good in me, something I had long lost sight of.

It was a lovely moment, but one that was fleeting, of course. One afternoon, I was out in the yard, working at the weight pile, when a watch commander approached me. "I need to speak with you," he said.

As he took me aside, I couldn't imagine what the issue might be. He told me that the Nevada prison system had a new guy "upstairs," and that he was making some changes. "They've got a lot of young gangbangers coming into Ely," he said, "and he's worried about violence here. So, his plan is to lock down the old-timers like you—guys with violent histories—to prevent problems. I guess he figures there's less of you than them, so fourteen of you guys will be going into lockdown as a precaution."

"As a precaution? But I didn't do anything!"

"They're saying it's for the safety and security of the institution."

"For how long?"

"Till they figure things out, I guess." He stared at the ground, and then looked up at me as if to say, "I'm only the messenger."

This was terrible. More than that, it was wrong. I had done nothing to warrant this punishment, yet for the "safety and security of the institution," I was being placed into solitary confinement. My job at the weight pile, my life in general population, and my relative freedom were all gone. There wasn't a thing I could do.

On February 3, 1992, thirteen of us "old-timers"—most in our thirties—were moved into solitary confinement cells to face a brutal existence: twenty-three hour a day containment in a concrete box, one hour out for rec a few times a week, twice-a-week showers, and a food tray passed through a flap in the door. For all out-of-cell trips, I would be strip-searched, cuffed, and shackled.

I was furious. I paced the small cell, growing hot with the unfairness of it. *I haven't done anything! I'm being punished for institutional convenience, that's what!*

But most disturbing was the vagueness of how long it would last. When I'd done hole time in the past, it had been for twenty-nine days, so I always knew when I'd be getting out. But this was different. *Till they figure things out?*

I immediately began sending out kites, asking the question, "How long?" I received a quick written response stating that my case was "under review" and that a decision would be made in ninety days. Existing in this cell for three months was a hell of a lot longer than the twenty-nine-day stints I'd known before, but there was nothing to do but endure it and wait.

In the meantime, I went out to rec at every opportunity, which wasn't even exactly outside. The recreation space was like a tall concrete box, but without a roof. Fortunately, several other "old-timers" were out there with me, so we got to talk, play cards, play handball, and rail against the unfairness of our situation.

The weeks crawled along until finally, the ninety-day mark was reached. As promised, a form was slid under my door. The review stated that, due to my violent history, I could not be released to the general population but that this decision would be reconsidered in another ninety days. I crumpled it up and threw it against the wall.

The next three months were hell. I had no radio, no TV, and no magazines, newspapers, or books, not even a Bible, to read. There was just nothing but a bunk, a toilet, and four walls. I tried to create some daily structure with exercise—jumping jacks, push-ups, and pacing the cell while I waited for the next ninety days to pass.

My only salvation was rec, where I got to be among others. It kept us connected; it kept me sane. But that, too, would soon be taken away. Because of several stabbings on days that I hadn't been outside, prison officials rescinded all human interaction. A new policy prohibited us from socializing with each other in the rec yard. We were to be taken out individually in separate shifts. I now stood alone in the rec yard and stared at the sky.

Despite my barrage of kites to prison administrators, the pat response was always the same: my case was "under review." And every ninety days, the results of the "review" were dutifully slid under my door. Each one stated the exact same reason for my elevated level of captivity: violent history. No one ever came to speak to me, and I doubt there was ever any actual review taking place. They were just checking off boxes. I was locked up like this because it made life easier for prison administrators, pure and simple.

I can't say how many ninety-day cycles came and went as I was losing all track of time. But I felt the heat of summer and the cold of winter, so I knew at least a year had passed. Sometimes, I would hear a different kind of footstep in the hall, and my heart would leap. Maybe I was about to be released, maybe I hadn't been forgotten. But then the footsteps receded and I slumped back on my bunk.

There was no end in sight—just more meaningless reviews. The loneliness was taking its toll. I found myself becoming more and more listless, not bothering with outside rec at all anymore. I sat on my bunk and stared. I had never realized the value of human connection. Even a little chitchat here and there would have helped. I so longed for someone to talk to. But there was nothing.

But with what little energy I could muster, I continued to fight back—not with my fists but with my pen. I stepped up on the kites, sending them out every single day. *"I didn't do anything! When? When will I be released from this hell? Please! Tell me when!"*

I sent the kites off to lieutenants, sergeants, correctional caseworkers—guards who supposedly showed a little interest in us. I sent them out to everyone and anyone I thought might listen.

CHAPTER 20

Hope Springs Eternal

There was a rapping on my door. A guard unlocked it and told me the warden wanted to see me. After I was searched, cuffed, and shackled, I shuffled through the halls till we reached his office.

The warden looked up from his desk. "Come in, Frank. Sit down."

I sat down across from him, and he said, "Listen, Frank, we're getting your kites, we're getting them, okay? I understand you want to go back to population."

"Yes, sir, I do."

"Okay, I have a deal to offer you. But I need you to show me something. So, here's what I want from you. You give me forty-five days of no problems, forty-five days with no fights, no write-ups, and you're out. Think you can do that?"

"Yes, sir. Yes, I can."

"All right then, I'll see you in forty-five days."

Finally! The end was in sight. Forty-five days? No problem! All I had to do was avoid the things that could lead to write-ups—sending cadillacs to other convicts, mouthing off at the guards, or putting a towel over my cell door window. A lot of guys did that when they used the toilet to create a little privacy, but that was technically an infraction.

I paced my cell as always, but now with excitement. In a month and a half, I'd be out of solitary and back on the yard. I'd be going to culinary with everybody else. Maybe I could get my job back. I started going back out to rec, practically whistling as guards shackled and cuffed me. When I got outside, I looked up at the sky and smiled. Back in my cell, I dropped my face into my hands and prayed to God, thanking him. It was almost over.

The first month of my commitment to Warden Wolff passed by smoothly. I ignored any provocations, greeted the guards amiably, and stayed so far inside the line that I was practically invisible. Two more weeks and this nightmare would end. The countdown had begun.

But one morning, just after breakfast, it all started to unwind. I heard the familiar rustle of footsteps and keys, and I stood at my cell door window and looked out. Three guards were in the hall, standing in front of the cell directly across from me. The cell belonged to a convict who had a pending lawsuit against some other guards. One of them motioned to the control booth at the end of the hall, requesting the door to be unlocked. I recognized him as Sergeant Hogan, one of the more dishonorable guards. When the door "popped," he waved the other two into the cell and stood back. I guess Hogan and his crew were going to persuade the convict to retract the lawsuit. While the guy was being pummeled, Hogan was glancing around to see if anyone was watching. Our eyes met. He nodded, and I nodded back.

A couple of days later, a guard showed up at my cell with an infraction ticket. He told me I was being written up for having a towel over my window. It was signed by Sergeant Hogan. In an instant, I knew exactly what the bastard was up to. If I'd had a towel over the window, I never could have seen what I saw, and if I was called as a witness to this assault, I'd be branded a liar, as the infraction ticket would "prove" I couldn't have seen a thing.

My blood was boiling. This ticket would destroy my hopes for liberation from this cell. I had to get it dismissed. I hovered at the window, watching for Hogan to come by. As soon as I spotted him, I called him over. "Sergeant, what's with this BS ticket?"

"Don't worry about it," he said.

"Listen, I can't get a write-up. I have a deal with the warden. He's going to let me out of here if I don't get any write-ups. I can't have this! Please!"

"Don't worry about it, De Palma. It ain't going anywhere."

"Look, I've been in this cell for over a year. I can't take it anymore. I need to get out. This ticket is BS!"

"I told you. It ain't going anywhere, don't worry," he said and walked away.

A few days later, I was called to a disciplinary hearing presided over by a lieutenant, a sergeant, and a couple of guards. It was at this point that the ticket would have been dismissed. I prayed that Hogan had seen to it. I hoped he had kept his word. "How do you plead?" I was asked.

"Not guilty," I said. "I did not have a towel over my window. Maybe he made a mistake. Maybe it was another cell."

The lieutenant instructed me to step out while they reached a decision. I stood in the hall and waited. A couple of minutes later, I was brought back in.

"Well, Mr. De Palma," the lieutenant said, "we all agree to rely on an officer's report, and we find you guilty. You'll be docked five days of recreation as punishment."

I felt like I'd been punched in the gut, my legs weakening underneath me. I left the hearing room in a panic. Hogan hadn't intervened at all! He'd done nothing. He'd lied to me—telling me it wasn't going anywhere.

The following day, I was escorted to the office of a disgusted warden, who was holding up the ticket, and my heart sank. "What's this that came across my desk?"

"No, Warden, it's not what you think it is."

"Not what I think it is? I see exactly what it is. It's a ticket for having a towel over your window. You know what I told you—forty-five days without issues and you'd get out. You couldn't give me forty-five days, De Palma?"

If there was ever a moment when I did not want to hold my mud, this was it. I wanted to spill it all, tell him exactly what happened. But I couldn't. The next cell-door visit would be mine. "It's not what you think, Warden," I stammered. "It's just not what you think."

I left his office, engulfed in anger. Hogan had lied to me, blown me off as I languished in that cell, and thought nothing of it. He could have easily had the phony ticket dismissed, but he never even bothered. Now, I might never get out of solitary. Perhaps even worse, I'd lost face with the warden, a man who'd believed in me, who'd let me hold his granddaughter. I would never let this go. Never! Hogan would not get away with it.

I hovered at my window, waiting for him to come by. My fury was settling into a coldness like I had never felt before. As soon as I saw him, I motioned him over.

"What's up, De Palma?" he said.

"You lied to me. You said nothing would come of that ticket. You lied."

He looked at me with an expression that read, "So what?"

I spoke these words calmly: "When I get the opportunity, I am going to kill you."

He jumped back, indignant. "You know, De Palma, threatening an officer is an infraction. I'm going to write you up for that."

"I mean it," I said as he walked away.

If he was smart, he would take me seriously. It took several months, but the passage of time only intensified my determination. I had to stand up for myself, for the injustice that had been done to me. I watched for him, and I waited.

Then the opportunity came. I was in a sally port, the secure plexiglass enclosure at the entryway to my unit that abutted the control bubble, where guards controlled the door locks on the unit. I was standing alone, handcuffed and shackled, waiting for an escort to take me to the clinic. Then I saw him coming down the hall, headed straight toward me. My belly chains had not been fastened securely, and I quickly stepped out of them and tucked the loose ends into my oranges. He entered the sally port, gave me a quick glance, and stood at the inside door, waiting for the guard in the control booth to open it. Without hesitation, I slipped the chains off, tossed them around his neck, and body slammed him to the floor.

"I told you, man! I told you!" I shouted as I pulled the chain tight. He was on his stomach, fighting hard as I pulled harder. Alarms and buzzers were going off. I pulled with everything I had, hampered by the handcuffs.

And then I heard a gun rack. I looked up to see the barrel of an M14 nosing out from the control bubble window, pointed at my head. "Let go of him—I will put one in your head."

I pulled the chain harder. And then an army was overpowering me, shouting, arms everywhere, pulling me off him. They grabbed him out from under me, got me on my feet, and commenced to beat the crap out of me till my legs gave out and my face was a bloody pulp. On the floor, they got me spread-eagled and a 400-pound guard stood on my head and bounced up and down. Then, in his steel-toed boots, he propped himself up on a ledge and, with everything he had, kicked me in the groin. After the third strike, everything went white.

When I woke up, I was lying on the infirmary floor, cuffed, shackled, and unable to see. My eyes were swollen shut. But I could hear the whispers:

"Who's that?"

"It's De Palma."

"Holy shit!"

It was clear to me they had no intention of providing any medical attention, so I lay there for a few days, falling in and out of consciousness. After that, I was lifted to a cot, where I remained for a good month as my body slowly healed.

That fit of rage landed me back in the courtroom, where I was charged with attempted murder. I did not fight it the way I had fought my murder charge years earlier. That was self-defense; this was not. I'd deliberately tried to kill the man. Another twenty or thirty seconds and he would have been gone. He did wind up with a broken collarbone, and I'd screwed up his shoulder and throat. But, in the end, Sergeant Hogan made a full recovery.

I was guilty as charged and sat passively, listening as my sentence was read: *twenty years*. Hogan was in the courtroom throughout the proceedings, and we never looked at each other. But after the sentence was passed and everyone stood up to leave, I looked at him directly and said loud enough for all to hear, "You shouldn't have done what you did, and you shouldn't have lied to me."

PART TWO

. . . looking down these dreary passages, the dull repose and quiet that prevails, is awful. . . a black hood is drawn; and in this dark shroud, an emblem of the curtain dropped between him and the living world, he is led to the cell from which he never again comes forth, until his whole term of imprisonment has expired . . . he is a man buried alive; to be dug out in the slow round of years . . .

—Charles Dickens, "American Notes for General Circulation"

CHAPTER 21

Treat as a Non-Human

After my sentence was passed, the prison administration ramped up my security classification. In a formal proceeding, I was brought into a hearing room that was packed with correctional staff of every level, who stared me down—the one who'd tried to kill one of their own.

The associate warden spoke, "Mr. De Palma, you are considered one of the three most unpredictable and violent prisoners in the Nevada system—if not *the* most violent. Based on your actions, we are reclassifying you to the highest security level—'High Risk Potential.' As an HRP, you will be dealt with accordingly." He looked at me and asked, "Is there anything you wish to say?"

I had only one thought: "For what it's worth, violence doesn't happen out of the blue. There's always something behind it. There's always something behind every violent act in this prison. That's all."

He gave me a perfunctory nod and continued, "You, and you alone, have dug yourself into a deep hole, Mr. De Palma, and it will be up to you to dig yourself out."

When the hearing concluded, with handcuffs and shackles snapped tightly in place, I was shuffled to the "HRP" unit, which was strictly solitary confinement. As we got closer to the cell, one of the guards hollered, "Is there a mattress in his cell?" When the answer was affirmative, he shouted, "Pull it out! He doesn't get a fuckin' mattress."

No sooner had the cell door slammed behind me than a copy of a memo addressed to the staff was slid under the door. In the subject line was my name, "Frank De Palma." To briefly summarize, it said, "Treat the above-named individual as a non-human." Additional orders mandated that I was never to be taken to the shower or rec without four CERT officers present. "CERT" was short for Correctional Emergency Response Team. These were guards of gargantuan proportions who were called in to quell uprisings. There was one final directive: Whenever I left the cell, in addition to shackles and cuffs, a dog collar was to be fitted around my neck. I was to be walked on a leash to my three allotted weekly showers and my daily hour of outside rec.

Their anger toward me had not abated in the least—nor mine toward them.

I looked around at the cell, a small concrete square with an overhead fluorescent light. Like my previous solitary cell, it had a tiny sink and toilet and a steel bunk welded to the wall—minus a mattress. A narrow vertical window looked out on the desert in the distance.

The cell was cold, and that night I wrapped myself up as best as I could in the state-issued blanket and laid down on the concrete floor and tried to fall asleep.

As the days passed, I managed as best I could, going out to rec despite the humiliating ordeal. There was always the matter of locating the CERT officers, who were often scattered about the facility on different details. Once they arrived, I was chained, shackled, and fitted with the dog collar for the degrading walk on the leash. I endured it with a thick skin, just grateful for a little time out of the cell. The rec yard was another concrete box, with the open sky above and no one in it but me. I noticed a pull-up bar, grabbed it, and did chin-ups for the hour.

The guards made a point of not speaking to me. But they still hassled me when they could. When I reached for my food tray through the door flap, they often poured hot coffee on my hands. After one scalding, I was able to splash a cup of milk back in the guard's face. As punishment, I was switched over to the "diet loaf" for sustenance. It was a barely edible substance designed to sustain life but little else. It tasted like smelly cardboard, and I refused to eat it. As days went by, I grew weak with hunger. I did not have the energy to go out for rec and was unable to do more than lie on the floor. It was a tug-of-war between me and them, and though I grew weaker, my stubbornness remained intact. Two weeks went by, and I lay there, feeling the approaching shadow of death. On day sixteen, without any explanation, regular food resumed.

A month came and went, and the solitude was wearing me down. I'd already done close to two years in solitary prior to my switch to this HRP cell, and I guess the loneliness was cumulative. I yearned for someone to talk to in a way I never had before.

But if I was alone in my cell, I was not alone on the unit, and it was noisy as hell. Others consigned to a similar punishment screamed, wailed, and shrieked in nearby cells. I shuddered at the sounds of madness. Their cries were unnerving and unrelenting, one man's screams enduring for hours on end. I struggled to block it out.

With no radio, TV, newspapers, or books, I had no diversions and no connection to the outside world. There was nothing but me and four walls. But I battled back against plunging spirits with a self-disciplined regimen. I had always been tidy, and upon waking, I would get up from the floor and straighten my cell. With no mattress and no bed to make, I would fold my blanket neatly and place it on the bare bunk. Next, I washed my face, and though I had no mirror, I shaved as best I could. I used a plastic fork to comb my hair. The only clothing I'd been allotted was the orange jumpsuit, a pair of boxers, a T-shirt, one pair of socks, and plastic flip-flops. I slept in the jumpsuit, and in the morning, I put on the boxers I'd washed out in the sink the night before. I requested a toothbrush and toothpaste, but there were no guarantees on that.

Then, it was on to my familiar routine of push-ups and sit-ups—hundreds of them, until I was sweat-soaked. After that, I would pace the cell, counting my steps, "One, two, three, four"—turn! The cell wasn't much bigger than a parking space so there wasn't far to go. "One, two, three, four"—turn! I would pace like that for hours on end—back and forth, back and forth. Finally exhausted, I would sit down and stare, sometimes getting up to look out the window at the changing shadows over the desert, watching day turn into night.

As the months droned on, the guards were getting lax. The CERT team didn't always show up for my showers or rec, and half the time the guards didn't bother with the dog collar. But my interest in leaving the cell was waning anyway. I was growing anxious and depressed. I was also becoming disoriented, having trouble distinguishing between day and night. It was becoming one big blur. I asked to see a doctor, who prescribed Klonopin. The medication helped with the anxiety and depression and also helped me with sleep, which was becoming difficult. I was grateful for this, as sleep was my refuge.

Each day, I awakened to what felt like a mountain of inertia and confusion. It was getting harder to get enthused about rec—just an outdoor version of the cell. But I had to try. And so I pushed myself out to the small enclosure and stared up at the sky. And then, one day, something terrifying happened. I was just starting my chin-ups when the walls of the enclosure seemed to be moving, closing in on me, like I was being crushed. I felt like my heart would explode from my chest. Was I having a heart attack? The space was getting smaller, and I banged on the door. "Help! Get me out of here!"

Fortunately, one of the more decent guards was on duty that day, and he unlocked the door quickly. But before he could cuff me, I took off, tearing down the hall as he chased after me, shouting for me to stop. But he needn't have worried. I wasn't going anywhere. The only thing I wanted was to get back into my cell. It was only after I was locked back inside that my body calmed down and my breathing returned to normal.

I'd never had a panic attack in my life, and I never really understood what it even meant. But now I did. It was indescribable. I was terrified to go out again and decided to skip rec, at least for the time being. But I still wanted to shower, and though I was nervous about it, I decided to take a chance. But no sooner had I begun the walk to the shower than it started up again—the walls in the hall were moving, closing in on me. It felt like the air itself was crushing me. I raced back to my cell.

At first, the guards thought I was being difficult, just trying to give them a hard time. But once they realized I was having panic attacks, they started messing with my head, threatening to pull me out, so they could have a little fun. "Hey, let's bring De Palma out," they would taunt, causing me to quiver in fear.

I would never go out to rec again. For that matter, showers were out. Birdbaths in my sink would have to do. For some reason, light started bothering me. It just felt too stimulating. I took a towel and stuffed it in the small window and then I flicked off the overhead fluorescent light for good. For some reason, I needed the cell to be as dark as possible; it was within this darkened cave that I felt safest.

As time wore on, I ached for human connection. It felt like an actual pain. The only people in my world were the guards and the nurse who came by each day with my medication, her only words being, "Mr. De Palma—pill call." I would reach through the door flap for the pills. Gradually, they all faded away as real people and became what seemed like stick figures.

But there was one exception, a man with a genuine interest in my well-being—the prison chaplain. His name was James Stogner. Prior to solitary, I had visited him in his office, where we had talked about spiritual matters and everyday matters. Despite having been warned by prison officials that I was dangerous, he took a chance and got to know me anyway. One day, after one of our talks, he referred to me as his friend. I was deeply touched. Along with being entrusted with holding the warden's granddaughter, it was one of the highlights of my life. And here he was now, in the solitary confinement unit, standing at the window of my cell door. "Frank, my friend, how are you?"

"Oh, holding up, Chaplain, holding up. Thank you for stopping by."

We would chat a little bit, before he asked if he might say a prayer for me. I bowed my head.

"Heavenly Father, please look upon your son, Frank . . ."

Seeing Chaplain Stogner's warm face in my window always gave me a lift. I was grateful for my friend. He was all I had. I had lost all touch with my family; I had not spoken with my mother in a couple of years, and even the intermittent calls with my dad had fallen off. Occasionally, I would get a letter that was probably from one of them, but I tore it up before I could even see who had sent it. To connect with my family was an unbearable agony. I blotted them out, hoping they'd forgotten about me and gotten on with happy lives.

And then, the unthinkable. It was 1996, and I had been in solitary confinement for four years when I received word that my mother had died. I didn't think it was possible to feel any darker than I already did, but with this news, it was like a trapdoor opened, and down I fell into an even deeper pit of despair.

Throughout my life, my mother had been my one and only lifeline to love. We'd written each other over the years, and we'd always planned that when I got out, I would live with her. Even though I knew I'd never get out, we still dreamed. Occasionally, we'd been able to arrange a phone call when she visited my aunt Margie. She would yell into the phone, "I love you, Frankie! You're my baby." I would shout back, "I love you, Mom!" even though I knew she couldn't hear me. Somehow, I thought life would be long enough for me to see her again. By some miracle, I imagined myself taking care of her in her later years, like a good son should. But, in the end, the only thing I had brought her was heartache. I could almost feel her stroking my brow when I was a boy. "You're my baby."

Now she was gone. In my grief, I had it out with God. *Why do you let good people die and you keep letting me live?* Losing my mom was unbearable, and I found my pulse and put a razor on it. After all those years of fighting the BMF to stay alive, now, at the age of forty, I would die by my own hand. In one swift move, I tore into the radial artery of my wrist. Blood shot out like a geyser. The smell of blood is a smell unto itself, like copper. After a minute or so, my stomach started tightening up real bad, and I doubled over. And then it passed, and a euphoria followed.

It was all right. It was all right now.

CHAPTER 22

A Penal Tomb

I opened my eyes and found myself lying in a hospital bed, hooked up to two bags of blood, one connected to each arm. The doctor told me I'd lost the maximum amount of blood possible to stay alive. He said I'd coded twice, and they'd even had a TOD—time of death—but a med student had found a faint pulse in my groin.

He was the cheery sort, business as usual, when he asked, "So, what's going on?"

"Bad moment, I guess."

"Are you going to do it again?"

I didn't answer.

Because my artery had been so badly damaged, a stainless-steel tube had to be surgically implanted to replace it. It was a couple of days before I was shipped back to Ely, where I was promptly returned to my cell. But the prison's mental health staff checked on me a little more, for about a day or two. They did increase my medication, and a psych lady stopped by.

"Hi, Mr. De Palma," she said. "How are we feeling?"

"Fine."

"Well, if you ever want to talk, send a kite, okay."

"Yup."

She was accompanied by a yawning guard. After they were gone, it occurred to me that I actually had more respect for the yawner. At least he didn't pretend to care.

As time marched on, so did life events, both inside and outside the prison. Unbeknownst to me, on October 5, 1998, Roderick Abeyta, the prosecution's big witness against me in my murder trial, was executed by lethal injection.

Eight years into my solitary confinement brought the turn of the century. While the world celebrated the year 2000, I sat entombed in a cell in Ely State Prison, without the slightest awareness of this milestone. A year later, the nation was stunned by the attack on the World Trade Center on 9/11. I had no idea.

Through it all, I remained in my darkened concrete box, never once leaving for rec or a shower. I took my birdbath each day, and on the occasions that I had a toothbrush, I brushed my teeth. My only reprieve was periodic visits from Chaplain Stogner. Other than that, I ate my meals and stared. The pacing and my exercise regimen had long ceased. At some point, they tossed me a mattress, although by then, I really didn't care.

Though I didn't realize it at the time, I was slipping away. I was so lonely and cut off from everything natural and normal that I sought to make friends with the beetles and potato bugs that crawled around my cell. I talked to them, and using my index finger, I gently petted them. When my food tray came, I always put out a little for them. They didn't seem interested in it, but that was okay.

One day, a ladybug made her way across the floor. Holding her on my thumb, I asked, "What's it like to be a ladybug?" Though I'd grown fond of her, I didn't think it was fair to keep her in captivity, so I sang to her: "Ladybug, ladybug, fly away . . ." and I flicked her into the air. But she never left. Maybe she wanted to stay with me. One morning I woke up and found her dead on the floor. I struggled not to cry.

Sitting alone in the darkness, I took flight from my

confinement, imagining myself out in the world, in a supermarket, of all places. I was thumping honeydew melons, checking them for ripeness. A pretty gal was doing the same, and we got into a little conversation. Just friendly, of course, but next thing you know, we're cracking jokes and having a good laugh.

Should I ask her out? I'd like to, but . . . what if she says no, and I wind up feeling stupid? Hmm . . . better to see if I run into her again. But meeting her was sure a lot of fun.

As I occupied a world beyond the cell, the next matter I faced wasn't a lot of laughs, but a serious concern. I was a married man and had family matters that needed my attention. A problem had developed: My lovely wife and I lived a happy life together with our son and the family dog, just the four of us. And then one day, I learned that my son was hitting the dog. This was very disturbing, and I could not allow it to continue. But what to do? Would I yell at my son? Berate him? Hit him? No, no, I would never do that. I loved him dearly, and I could never hurt my child. But why was he doing this? I needed to understand it, and I needed to convey to him that it was not okay. I puzzled over it, trying to come up with just the right message, the right way to handle it. But it seemed that no matter how I played it out in my head, the right message eluded me. Consumed with my determination to be a good and loving father, I pondered this incessantly.

For how long I sat and pondered, muttering aloud to invisible scenarios that never existed nor would ever exist, I cannot say. Days? Weeks? Years? Time had lost all meaning, but these fantasies seemed like they went on forever. Looking back, it was probably close to a year. During this time, my hand robotically reached for the food tray. Out in the hall, I had a vague awareness of guards laughing at me. "Hey, you hear De Palma in there? He's gone, man! He's gone—ha, ha, ha!"

I can't say when or why reality crashed through, but in one horrifying moment, I realized there was no supermarket, no lovely wife, no son, and no dog. It was just me, Frank, staring at four concrete walls. *God help me!* I shrieked and cried aloud, joining in with the other voices of madness.

CHAPTER 23

Beginning of the End

In 2004, twelve years after I'd been in solitary confinement, I received a reprieve of sorts. I was taken off HRP (High Risk Potential) status. What this meant was that if I came out of my cell, the dog collar directive was removed, as was the order requiring the presence of CERT officers to escort me down the hall. This might have been a little more meaningful if I ever came out of the cell, but since I didn't, it hardly mattered. But what it did signal to me was a softening attitude toward me, one that I hoped might lead to a release from isolation.

In the early days of my lockdown, during the time I had been placed in solitary for the safety of the institution, I had relentlessly sent out kites requesting to be released back to general population. But in the years after my attack on Sergeant Hogan, I didn't bother; I knew it would be futile. But now, this change in my security status gave me a little hope. Yes, I had tried to kill a guard, but my punishment was an additional twenty years in prison. In a human lifespan, twenty years is a long time, a most substantial punishment. Not to mention that they'd beaten me to the brink of death. I couldn't really blame them for that. But now I needed to know when this torment would end. Composing these notes focused my mind somewhat, and I began sending them to the warden, asking the question, "When?" I sent a kite every single day. It had been twelve long years. I was desperate for an answer—desperate to know when I'd be released from hell.

And then, the answer finally came. I can't be sure of the date, but I believe it was 2005. It came in a visit from the warden himself. I could see him from the window of my door. His name was E.K. McDaniel. He was huge, probably weighing in around four hundred pounds. I watched him as he huffed and puffed his way toward me, all red-faced and scowling. When he reached my door, he stood for a moment, catching his breath. Then he looked at me through the window and said, "Mr. De Palma, I've been receiving your kites, asking when you'll get out of here. And I'm here to tell you that as long as I'm in charge, there are only two ways you're getting out. Either you get released from prison—and we both know that'll never happen—or you come out in a box. Do you understand me?"

I nodded. "Yes, sir. Yes."

As I watched him turn and shuffle away, my state of mind was so degraded that all I could think was that this important man had come to my cell—in person. I felt kind of privileged.

I don't know that I fully comprehended his message—that I was to exist within these four cement walls until my heart eventually stopped beating. I was forty-seven years old. But I do know that, after his visit, I never sent another kite.

CHAPTER 24

Buried Alive

When I entered prison at eighteen years old, I had hope—hope of going home in two years. But as new sentences began piling up, my hopes kept downgrading until my dreams and most of my life had eked away. My very last gasp of hope was that I would not die in prison. But even that would not be realized. This cell was my tomb, and I believed it was here that I would draw my final breath.

It was not only a death sentence that E.K. McDaniel had handed me, but it was a sentence meant to be carried out slowly and torturously. I would never converse or laugh with anyone again. I was to be alone, forever, doomed to an existence within my own head while I waited on my body to die.

The years in solitary continued, day into night, night into day—which was which, I had no idea. I knew nothing beyond the ever-deepening valleys of depression and the ravages of my deteriorating brain. When the Klonopin I was taking was removed from the prison formulary, I was switched over to Valium, but not before I lay on the floor, writhing through a miserable withdrawal. The Valium was not as effective, but then again, there is no drug in the world that can ease the agony of solitary confinement.

Though I no longer had any sense of time, the changes in my body told me that time was grinding on. I had no mirror, but when I ran my fingers through my hair, there was a lot less of it. My unused joints ached, and I was doubled over in back pain, all of which I tried to ignore. I had no choice. But one thing could not be ignored: an angry, throbbing tooth. It was a pain like none other, and I was dazed by it. Instinctively, I knew the tooth had to come out. But how? I did not have the mental wherewithal to put together a kite to request to see a dentist. It was beyond me. And even if I did, there was the matter of leaving my cell, which was out of the question. Horrific as the pain became, the thought of a panic attack was worse. No, I had to do it myself. It was the only way.

Using a nylon string that I pulled from the mattress, I worked it up into the gums and root of the molar. I tightened the string and tugged at it—back and forth, back and forth. My mouth kept filling up with squishy pus that I spit out in the sink. It took hours of working it like this, but finally, the tooth gave and was out. I rinsed out my mouth and fell onto my bunk in relief. Despite my horrific circumstances, the release of that tooth was a moment of joy. In the years to come, I would be forced to pull three more.

After fifteen years had passed, my existence was one of agony. Loud, shrieking voices filled my every waking moment. When they first started, I thought they were coming from out in the hall. But in a horrifying moment, I realized they were coming from inside of me. I tried everything to make them stop—singing, shaking my head back and forth, covering my ears—but the screams wouldn't let up. Sleep brought a little relief, but nightmares woke me, and I could no longer discern if I was asleep or awake. Driven to madness, I banged my head against the concrete wall, again and again and again. Blood ran down my face, but I kept at it, desperate to make the voices stop.

I can't say for how long I banged my head like that, but the voices eventually faded as I broke away from it all—the screams, along with all thoughts, feelings, and memories. I lay on my bunk and stared, peering into levels of darkness, each one with a deeper emptiness to it. It was different from the darkness of night. This darkness had a substance to it. As I entered an arena of nothingness, a catatonic state, I was becoming unglued, just atoms that were parts and pieces of nothing.

The years from 2006 to 2013 are gone to me. I became nothing more than an arm reaching for a food tray. I was later told that several people, both prisoners and civilians, including Chaplain Stogner, had come to my cell to see me, but that I never reacted to their knocks or to my name being called. My body was still there, but I was not.

While I remained in this state, on October 18, 2011, the United Nations addressed the issue of solitary confinement. Their Special Rapporteur on Torture, a man named Juan Méndez, asserted that the practice of solitary confinement could amount to torture. In a delivery to the UN General Assembly's committee that deals with humanitarian issues, he said, "Considering the severe mental pain or suffering solitary confinement may cause, it can amount to torture or cruel, inhuman, or degrading treatment . . ." Furthermore, he said that solitary confinement beyond fifteen days should be prohibited. The year the UN assumed this "fifteen-day" position, I had been in solitary confinement for nineteen years.

Although this United Nations decree would receive significant press coverage, it is unknown whether it came to the attention of the Nevada Department of Prisons. Most likely it did, but more likely, they simply ignored it.

For reasons I will never understand, after about seven years in an existence of nothingness, I started coming back together. The first thing I became aware of was lights going on and off in the hall. Though everything was foggy, I started to realize where I was.

"No!" I cried out. "Oh, God, no! I can't take this anymore. I can't be alone in here anymore. I don't want to feel anymore. I can't."

And then a voice came to me, and I heard these distinct words: *You are not nor have you ever been alone. Be still.*

To this day, I maintain that I clearly heard those words. But whose words were they? Was God finally showing himself to me? Or was the voice a manifestation of my insanity? I will never know. But in the next instant, I felt infused with something warm and comforting, like a cushiony marshmallow. I was no longer in a cell, but happily floating and tumbling in a good space, a safety net set out before me. I'll never understand it, but whatever happened, it held me, and it helped me.

As I came back to life, I remembered my family. My mom was gone, that I knew. But what about my dad? From a well deep within, I felt a strong urge to speak with my father, and I requested a phone call, which was granted.

I don't recall my first words to him, but I do remember being surprised by the strange sound of my own voice. "Frank, what's the matter with your voice?" my dad asked.

I hadn't spoken aloud in years, and my voice was garbled and weird sounding, but I could still be understood.

I learned my dad was ailing. He was also frantic. "Frank, son, was all this my fault? Was it my fault?"

"Aww, Dad, what are you talking about?"

"Can you forgive me, Frankie? Can you ever forgive me?"

"Sure, Dad, sure."

The phone system allotted fifteen minutes, but for some reason, it was malfunctioning that day, which worked in our favor. When the fifteen-minute mark was reached, it made a *faloop* noise and twice reset for another fifteen minutes, giving us forty-five minutes for what would be our final conversation.

"I need to know you're okay, son, that you're going to be okay. I need to know that you're okay."

"Of course I'm okay, Dad. I've got your blood coursing through my veins. How could I not be okay?"

The phone finally cut off, but not before he told me he loved me.

"I love you too, Dad."

A couple of days later, three guards showed up at my cell, offering to take me to the clinic. They said I needed to call my family.

But I already knew. "My dad died?"

Two of them stood poker-faced, but the third one nodded.

"No need." I went back to my bunk, closed my eyes, and returned to nothingness. I instinctively felt my body dying. It wouldn't be much longer now.

CHAPTER 25

22 Years and 36 Days

The date was March 11, 2014, and the knocking was getting louder, more insistent. It must have been going on for a while before it even registered that my name was being called. "Mr. De Palma!"

Go away! I thought.

"Mr. De Palma, it's Bill Johnson. I'm the psychologist here at Ely."

Bill Johnson? The name struck a note in some ancient reservoir of memory. But I couldn't really connect it, and it didn't matter anyway. Besides, I didn't know if this was real or if I was imagining it. I turned on my bunk and closed my eyes.

"Listen! We have some exciting news for you, Mr. De Palma. You're getting out of prison. Did you hear that? Your sentences are expiring. You're going to be paroled. We've got to be sure you're okay to be around people again. We've got to get you ready. We're moving you to the psych unit at the Northern Nevada Correctional Center."

I opened my eyes and implored them in my thoughts, *Just go away!*

Another voice called out, "Hey, Frank! This is Officer Greco. I've got Officer Price here with me. Look, Frank, we're not here to hurt you. We're not here to fight you. We just want you to come out, that's all. It's been a long time, man."

I pulled myself up on my bunk, realizing that these were real people speaking to me. Bits and pieces of what they were saying were coming together, making sense. But most of it wasn't.

"Something's broken inside you, and these people at the Northern Nevada Correctional Center are going to fix it. Okay, Frank?"

I lay back down, retreating into the familiar abyss of nothingness, hoping they would just leave.

"We don't like the things you did," Greco continued, "but dammit, Frank, you took it all, just like you gave it. You never complained or filed any grievances or anything. You've earned our respect—that's why Price and I volunteered to come up here and get you out."

I got up and stumbled to the door. I tried to tell them I was fine and to leave me alone. But what came out of my mouth was garbled mush. My vocal cords were not cooperating. I retreated to my bunk.

"Frank, we have to move you. How about I come in, grab your property, and we'll get you down to the transport van? You're getting out of prison, Frank."

I stood up, stretched out my arms, and started spinning around in circles. *Prison? I was in prison?* I didn't know what to think, where to start. *Getting out? What?!*

A flash of memory came to me, a man coming to see me—a big fat guy. He was all red-faced. "Listen to me, De Palma, and listen good—only two ways you're coming out," he'd said. "Either you get released from prison, and we know that'll never happen—or you come out in a box."

I had given up a long time ago.

Just go away!

The hollering continued. "What do you say, Frank? We've been out here for a while now. We're not going to force you out, okay?"

My brain was starting to click, rusted gears beginning to

turn. I kept spinning, patches of memory starting to connect, my cell starting to look familiar to me. I seemed to remember walking this cell before, a long time ago—walk four paces, hit the wall, turn, four paces back, hit the wall, turn. What happened? When had the pacing stopped? I didn't know. I'd been in the hospital. I'd cut myself bad. When was that? I had no sense of time. I ran my hand across my head. My hair was completely gone. I ran my tongue around my mouth, feeling gaps where teeth had been. Then I remembered the tooth pain; there was no forgetting that. I'd pulled them out myself. Took some doing, but I'd gotten them out. Lucky I'd even had a mattress when I'd needed the thread. I vaguely remembered way back, having no mattress, and sleeping on the floor. Huge chunks of time had passed.

The shouting started up again.

"Mr. De Palma!"

"Frank! Frank!"

"You're getting out of prison!"

Oh my God! Just go away! Leave me be! Please!

But they weren't leaving. How long they'd been out there, I didn't know.

"Listen, Frank," Greco hollered, "we've been standing out here for over seven hours now—that's right, seven hours! Will you let me come in, Frank? Will you let me help you? Come on, Frank."

Oh, God! I didn't know what to do. But one thing was getting through to me—they weren't going away.

"Okay, Frank," Greco said. "I can see you through the window. You're on your feet, you're doing good. You ready? You ready now?"

I must have nodded yes because the turnkey unlocked, and Greco swung the door open. Light flooded the darkened cell. I threw up my arms to cover my eyes. *Agghhh!*

He quickly shut it. "It's okay, Frank, it's okay. We'll take it a step at a time. I'm going to put the belly chains on you now."

The chains were familiar, almost reassuring. *Hurry, get them on!*

"Hey, what's this?" he said, reaching up to the window where I'd stuffed a towel some twenty years earlier. He tugged on it, and it disintegrated into a fine powder that swirled in the air. "What the hell?" he cried.

But with the towel gone, light was streaming through the window now, and panic was welling up inside. *What are you doing to me?*

"Shut your eyes, Frank, just shut your eyes," Greco commanded. "Here, hold on to me," he said, tucking my hand into his belt. "Now, we're going to the end of the hall and down a set of stairs, where they're going to get you into the transport van."

I was gasping for air, unsure how much longer my legs would hold me up.

"Just hold on to me, and we'll take it slow. Okay, now, let's go."

With Officer Greco leading the way, I shuffled out of the only place I'd known for the past two decades—a dank cell inside Nevada's Ely State Prison.

Officer Price grabbed me on the other side, and I squeezed tight to Greco's belt. With my eyes shut, I couldn't see them, but a little crowd had gathered. I could make out the whispers:

"He's out."

"It's Frank De Palma."

"How long was he in that cell? Twenty years?"

"No—twenty-two years . . ."

"What?! Twenty-two years ago, I was a baby . . ."

"Oh my God!"

Apparently, getting me out was a team effort that included not only Officer Greco, Officer Price, and Dr. Johnson, but an associate warden, another psychologist, and some mental health nurses. Two CERT officers stood by in case I caused any problems. Fat chance!

Now, they were all walking beside me, talking to me, encouraging me. I tried to say something back, but once again, the only thing that came out of my mouth was mush.

"What did he just say? What?"

I just didn't know how to make my voice work.

Sweat poured over me, and I panted for air, shuffling only a few feet at a time before I needed to rest. They were expecting me to walk further than I'd walked in decades.

I can't do it.

"It's okay, Frank, you're doing fine."

But I wasn't doing fine. The light, the open space, and all these people were terrifying. *Too much!* I turned to go back.

"No, no, you're almost there, Mr. De Palma." I recognized Bill Johnson's voice. "It'll all be better once you get to NNCC. I promise you, it's going to get better."

I caught my breath, clenched my eyes tighter, and kept shuffling.

"Almost there, almost there," everyone was saying.

Down the stairs we went, slowly.

"We got him now," two unfamiliar voices said.

I let go of Greco and Price, and two transport officers took over, walking me into a holding cell and shoving me into a chair. Any courtesies that had been shown me by Officer Greco would not be afforded by these two. They slapped on the handcuffs and ratcheted them so tight that I threw my head back and screamed in pain. Next came a black box that went over the cuffs for extra measure, and they tightened them up some more.

Aagghhhh!

As I gasped for air, a nurse ran in and jabbed me with a sedative.

"Don't worry, De Palma," one of them joked. "They'll take 'em off when you get to NNCC."

"Yeah," the other one laughed. "It's only a six-and-a-half-hour drive."

But while the two of them were getting their kicks out of torturing me, I was grateful for the distraction of pain. On the drive to the Northern Nevada Correctional Center, I held my eye on the swelling mass of flesh around the cuffs. Focusing on it held back something far worse—a tsunami of anxiety . . . sheer panic.

PART THREE

It never hurts to see the good in someone.
They often act better because of it.
—NELSON MANDELA

CHAPTER 26

A Force Like None Other

When they pulled me out of the van at the Northern Nevada Correctional Center, the only thing I cared about was getting back inside a darkened cell. I was taken to an intake area, where the black box and cuffs were removed. The nurses looked askance at the sight of my bloody, swollen wrists, while the guards grinned. From there, I was moved to a "suicide cell" for one night as a precaution. What this meant was that bright fluorescent lights shone down on me all night long. It was practically unbearable. After twenty years without light exposure, this was an absolute assault on my senses, and getting through that night was a horror.

Thankfully, the next morning, I was taken to my cell. It was not as dark or as small as I would have liked, but as I stumbled through the door on legs that didn't feel like they were mine, it was still an enormous relief.

Over the next few weeks, I stayed cocooned inside. The first thing I did was stuff a towel in the window to block out the light. No one seemed to notice or care what I did. Despite all the talk that there was something broken inside me that needed fixing, other than a continuation of my daily dose of Valium, no other type of support emerged. I would later learn that the only reason I was released from solitary was because psychologist Bill Johnson had warned that if I was to be released from solitary directly to the streets when my prison sentence ended, I'd be dead in a week or on *World News Tonight*. I guess that made them a little nervous.

But other than pull me out of that cell and dump me in the psych unit at the Northern Nevada Correctional Center, there was no plan. The only difference between my solitary cell at Ely and my new cell here was that this door was popped open at different intervals during the day, affording me the freedom to go in and out at will—not that I had any intention of going anywhere.

I struggled to piece together everything that was happening, but my brain was in a fog, and I couldn't make sense of much. I could not connect my thoughts in any logical way, and I stopped trying. All I really wanted was to curl up in my bunk and stay asleep.

But after a couple of weeks went by, I grew restless. I understood that things were a little different now. I eyed the door and knew it could be opened, not that I wanted to open it. The very thought of open spaces, noise, light, and being around people set my heart pounding and my palms sweating. But it was also dawning on me that I could not go on like this. If outside help was not forthcoming, then it would be up to me to help myself.

In the beginning, I spent days staring at the door, imagining myself just opening it. One day, I put my hand on the knob and turned it, before racing back to my bunk. About a week later, I experimented with simply opening and shutting the door. That was all I could manage.

Bit by bit, I grew comfortable with this routine. The next agony I faced was going out the door and leaving the safety of the cell. One morning, in a fit of courage, I forced myself to walk down the hall to the dayroom. It was only for a moment before I ran back. But I was a little excited. Each day, I would venture out to the dayroom where I washed a table down with a rag, all the while counting, "One, two . . ." before I dropped the rag and took off. It was like holding your breath—you can only do it for so long. After I'd managed two seconds, I aimed to make it "three." But when I tried for "four seconds," the panic rose, the walls started moving in, and I raced back.

I'd never experienced these mental disorders prior to solitary confinement, but they did not dissipate in its aftermath. I was told by a nurse that I was now suffering from agoraphobia. It was brutal. I went to sleep at night praying morning wouldn't come, as I would once again face "the door." Some days, it was just too much, and I didn't try. On others, I was able to increase the time until I got into double digits. My goal was to remain out of my cell for one whole minute.

As I ventured out more, some of the guards and staff spoke to me, just basic "good mornings," things like that. I pushed myself to reply in kind. At first, the sounds that came out of my mouth were still those raspy bits of garble, followed by a scratchy throat. But as I kept at it, my speech improved, and even though I didn't feel normal inside, at least I started sounding a little better.

If I knew what I sounded like, I had yet to see what I looked like. It had been decades since I'd seen myself in a mirror, and I dreaded the moment I knew was coming. I constantly examined my withered hands and ran my fingers across my bald pate in disbelief. What had happened to my full, thick head of hair?

A nurse told me that I was fifty-eight years old. The number shocked me. The last number I remembered was thirty-five—the age I entered solitary. Where had my life gone? Finally, the moment came when a nurse placed a mirror into my shaky hands. I looked into it and gasped. Staring back at me was a bald, stooped, toothless old man. Tears rolled down my cheeks. *This can't be me—it just can't.* When I'd entered solitary, I was in my prime, benching 460 pounds. That's how I'd remembered myself. I asked her to take the mirror away. I never wanted to look in the mirror again.

As the months wore on, the battle within me to come out of that cell and face the world, as it was, continued. But I was making progress. I was able to withstand longer and longer periods of "outside" time. My thoughts were also coming together in ways that started making sense. As my mind became clearer, I turned my focus to the med cart that appeared at my cell door every afternoon with my dose of Valium. I'd been taking Valium for twenty years, and I was tired of it. I didn't like being dependent on drugs. I had always steered clear of the illicit drugs that flooded the Nevada State Prison, and although Valium was perfectly legal, I told the doctors that I'd had enough. But they said because I'd been on it for so long, I would probably need it for the rest of my life. I would not accept this, so they agreed to wean me down and see how it went.

Every two weeks the dosage was reduced, and when it was brought down to 20 mg, I was done. They said it was too soon, but not one more pill would I take. I was confident in my decision. A brutal withdrawal set in, worse, I was told, than kicking heroin. I lay on the floor of my cell, my stomach lurching, my body sweating and convulsing. As the seizures worsened, the medical staff urged me to resume the Valium, warning that this could kill me. But I'd come this far, and I wasn't turning back. After a good two weeks passed, the seizures lessened, and my stomach started settling until, one morning, I woke up in the mood for breakfast. My twenty-year addiction to Valium was over. One of the guards made a point of telling me that although he didn't like me, he admired me for getting through it. I have to admit feeling a little proud of myself. It was a victory.

After a couple more months on the Northern Nevada Correctional Center psych ward, a half-hearted therapist called me into his office and told me that because I was being released, they needed to be sure I was okay to be around people. This was the first reference to release that I'd heard since that horrible walk down the hall at Ely. His words echoed Bill Johnson's concerns that I function normally among people. This therapist's idea was that I join a weekly group therapy session with the other patients on the unit. I told him I was fine with it. Anything that might help me.

A few days later, I sat down in a circle of prisoners with serious psychiatric disorders, where it was immediately obvious that this group couldn't do anything for me. With long dirty beards and filthy clothes, these prisoners were the sickest of the sick. It was as though I was trading the madness of solitary for a new type of madness. It was all very confusing. The things they said were fragmented and nonsensical. But I paid attention to every word. My own induced psychosis at this very same facility some thirty-five years earlier, under the directives of the evil Dr. Freeman, had left an indelible impression on me, as had the psychosis I developed in solitary. I knew what insanity felt like. I understood the struggle of trying to organize your own brain. It was inexplicable. It was terrifying.

As I struggled to make sense of what these poor souls were trying to communicate, I couldn't fathom why they were here in the first place. They were not the drug dealers and gang-bangers that dominated prison yards. They were different. As they sputtered incoherently and believed they were aliens, I couldn't imagine how they could be held responsible for anything. Not only were they in prison, but they were kept in the most miserable circumstances imaginable. Except for this weekly session, they were locked in their cells twenty-four seven, where they were pretty much out of it. No radios, no TVs, no nothing. It was just like solitary confinement, except they hadn't done anything to warrant it; they'd just been cursed with the cruelest of illnesses.

In the late afternoon, just as they were starting to come to life, nurses came by with pills that zapped them out again.

They never got out to rec, never got haircuts, and never showered, shaved, or enjoyed the most basic prison amenities, like a few commissary items. Even if they had a few dollars in their accounts, they were simply incapable of navigating the system. They needed a little help to figure out the shower schedule and such, but no efforts were made to accommodate them. Bored nurses did little more than dole out meds and stare at the clock while the guards did pretty much the same. Nobody gave a shit.

But it bothered me that they couldn't even take a shower. And despite their compromised states, I could tell that it bothered them, too. My own mental state was still quite fragile, but I worked up my nerve and started sending kites to the warden, describing the situation and asking that arrangements be made to help these people. Helping them gave me a focus, a mission of sorts, and a further incentive to push myself. During weekly therapy, I told the group about my request to the warden. Now and again, the wires of their brains came together, and I could see that they grasped it. I could also see they were a little hopeful.

I started getting responses to my kites, basically telling me the officers in the unit were doing their best and were already overworked. I shot back that they were standing around, drinking coffee.

Naturally, my complaints did not sit well with the guards, who told me to mind my own business. I kept at it anyway. But nothing changed, and the patients became frustrated and confused, irrationally blaming me for the inaction. One guy spat a fat loogie in my face. As I wiped away the spittle, anger did not rise in me the way it would have under other circumstances. A particularly angry guy named Sonny flung urine and feces at me when I passed by his cell. "Oh, Sonny," I cried, "come on, man." But it never crossed my mind to raise my hands to him. This was different.

The guards were getting irritated with me and started retaliating by going through my cell, searching for weapons. There were none. After all I had been through over the past decades in solitary, weapons and shanks were the last thing on my mind. But it didn't matter to them. One guard in particular made it his business to search my cell every single day, verbally provoking me while he was at it. By now, I was just feeling old and tired.

"Look," I said, "there's nothing you can do to me that hasn't been done. Nothing. Do whatever you want. I don't care."

My personal mission to help the psychiatric patients at the Northern Nevada Correctional Center got exactly nowhere. But I did get an unexpected reward. On one of his more lucid days, Sonny beckoned me to his cell door. "Frank, Frank, you got a minute?"

"Yeah, Sonny, what's up, man?"

"If I were you, I would kill me. I throw piss and shit at you. But you don't get mad at me. You know, Frank, you're a good friend."

I looked at this poor man, and my heart broke. "Thank you, Sonny."

One of the more decent guards noted my efforts and actually paid me a compliment, telling me that I was altruistic toward defenseless people. I kind of liked that. But he was the exception; the others had had enough and claimed my efforts were not altruistic but were motivated by a secret plan to convert the psychiatric unit into my own gang.

That did it. After ten months on the Northern Nevada Correctional Center psych ward, I had to get out. Though I hadn't fully recovered from my ordeal in solitary and suspected I never would, I also knew there was nothing at this place that was going to help me any further. I'd gotten myself out of that cell on my own, and I'd kicked Valium on my own. Now I needed to get the hell out entirely. But where to go? Being a maximum-security prisoner, I figured my only option was a return to Ely, hopefully to the general population. I was not thinking clearly at all, but my mind was made up. I had to get out.

But no sooner had I submitted my transfer request than things took a most unexpected turn. I was summoned to an administrative office, where I was confronted by the Northern Nevada Correctional Center's associate warden, a woman named Lisa Walsh.

"Mr. De Palma!" she shouted. A fiftyish woman, she had a loud, commanding presence.

"Yes, ma'am!"

"You're getting out of prison. You're going home. Why do you want to go back to Ely?"

I was not familiar with female corrections authorities and didn't quite know what to make of this woman. But beyond that, I was skeptical of this "going home" talk and told her so.

"Mr. De Palma, I promise you, you're due to be paroled. Your sentences are expiring. Unless you do something stupid, your release date is set for June 21, 2018."

June 21, 2018. This was the first solid information I'd heard thus far. I still didn't quite buy it. But even if it was true, 2018 was a few years off, and I could not take it any longer in this facility, and I explained that to her.

"Ely would be a mistake," she said. "That would be going in the wrong direction. I think it would be better for you to move off the psych unit and into the general population here at NNCC. Your release will be here before you know it. You better start getting ready."

"But Miss Walsh," I protested, "NNCC is medium security. I'm a max classification."

"Why don't you let me worry about that?"

She was a force like none other, and although I didn't know it at the time, meeting Miss Walsh would mark a true turning point in my life. After that encounter, she started keeping tabs on me, getting on my case if I stayed in my cell too much. I told her I was doing the best I could, which did not satisfy her in the least.

A couple of weeks later, it was official: I had been reclassified for medium security. I don't know what strings this woman pulled, but I would be going to the general population yard at the Northern Nevada Correctional Center. I could scarcely believe it. Then again, I was starting to believe, because there was something different about this lady. She meant what she said, and she got things done. I was secretly relieved that I wasn't going back to Ely and kind of excited about staying here. But the best part was that I would remain under her watch. She might have been a little gruff, but that was okay as she seemed genuinely interested in my well-being—a first in my forty-year prison ordeal.

A couple of days before I left the psych ward for general population, Miss Walsh quietly pulled me aside, telling me there was something she needed to say. I couldn't imagine what it might be.

"You know, De Palma, I owe you an apology."

"For what?"

"For what we did to you. I heard about you a long time ago. I knew you were inside that cell at Ely. What we did to you was terrible."

"You didn't do anything, Miss Walsh."

"I should have done something. We should have done something."

"A lot of people should have done something."

"I'm sorry," she said.

I was stunned. She was the only person to apologize, the only one to acknowledge the atrocity of my solitary confinement. I would savor her words forever.

CHAPTER 27

Seeing the Good

The difference between a maximum- and medium-security facility is as wide as the Grand Canyon. Medium smelled clean, whereas the stench in max was sweaty and bloody. The guards were calm, and the air—it was just lighter than the hardness of max. I couldn't help but wonder how I might have fared had I been placed in a medium facility when I was eighteen. Maybe I would have been in and out. I tried not to think about it. What was the point?

Oddly enough, an easier prison existence was still an adjustment. I arrived in the general population on a cold day in January 2015. I was pushing a cart with my meager belongings, headed for a housing unit on the far side of the yard. Midway across, I stopped, suddenly realizing I was unescorted. Something was wrong. I turned around, and a few guards were looking at me. I glanced up at the gun tower, where the guard was also watching. There had been people in the yard earlier, but now it was empty.

A setup? This was a setup! I shoved the cart aside. "Fuck you!" I shouted at the tower. "You're going to shoot me in the back? Come out here and get me like a man!"

But they all just looked at me blankly. A convict I'd known years earlier at the Nevada State Prison was running out to me. "It's okay, Frank, it's okay. You're in medium now. You don't need an escort here. You can walk by yourself. The yard is empty because everyone went in for chow, that's all."

One of the guards walked over to me. "Relax, man. Relax."

My entire body was shaking. They had no idea how overwhelming this was for me. All I'd known in prison was life and death, with nothing in between. Couple that with the terror I felt at the giant open space of the yard. In that moment, it was all too much.

Although my fear of open spaces and of being around people persisted, as I settled into life in Northern Nevada Correctional Center's general population, things improved, and the outdoors became a powerful draw. It often felt like a tug-of-war waging inside me—a pull between crippling anxiety warning me against leaving my cell and my desire to go outside and turn my face to the sun. More often than not, sunshine won the day.

Thankfully, my legs were working well again, and I walked the yard like a man in a happy trance. The yard was so familiar, especially the weight bench. I well remembered that, just prior to solitary, I had qualified for the "400 Club." I knew I could no longer lift anywhere near four hundred pounds, but I ran to the weights anyway to relive old times. But it would not be at all as I remembered it. I lay down on the bench and got under the bar, and something was wrong. I had no push or pull strength. The bar just came down on my chest. The strength and vitality of my youth was forever gone. It hurt.

But this loss was offset by new interests. The Northern Nevada Correctional Center offered a variety of activities. It was all so different here. One of them was gardening. I'd never had any interest in gardening before, but for some reason, I became enchanted with the flowers and happily learned all about tending a garden. I weeded and watered the marigolds and sunflowers, feeling like a regular person. It was a great joy, and I also think it was rather healing. As I dug my hands into the earth each morning, my former world of hatred and violence grew further and further away. I rather liked this new way of being.

But if my days as a fearsome fighter were behind me, my reputation as such was still very much alive. Although I had been locked away for over two decades, the guards, most of whom were children when I entered solitary, treated me with extreme caution. And when I walked the yard, I walked alone. It seemed the other prisoners were steering clear of me. But when a few brave souls approached me and struck up a conversation, it was as if a dam broke. These young kids started running up to me, all wide-eyed. "You're Frank De Palma? Man, you're a legend—you're Frank the shank!"

One of them told me he'd been hearing all about me. "When I was in juvie," he said, "they kept telling us, 'Keep acting that way, and you're going to wind up in prison with Frank De Palma, and he's going to kill you.'"

One of the guards told me that during his corrections training, my name was used as an example of how to deal with an extremely dangerous convict. He said they used me as a training tool. "They would say to us, 'This is how he does it; this is what De Palma does to people.'"

All of this came as a surprise to me. And it also made me sad. This was not the notoriety I sought. I was not born to hurt people. I fought because I had been backed into a corner. This was never the life I would have chosen for myself. I had wanted a life like everybody else's—a family, career, children, grandchildren. But for whatever reason, it wasn't meant to be, and I did my best with the hand I was dealt in the only way I knew how.

But now, I was in a far different place, ready to put it all behind me and move on. With Miss Walsh's support, I had a chance. She was urging me to prepare for release, and I was trying. One nagging worry was my hep C diagnosis. Although I felt okay, I knew the virus was running rampant in my body.

While I hadn't been interested in treatment in my twenties, I wanted it now. I discussed it with Miss Walsh, who told me that hep C treatment had come a long way since I'd met with that doctor at the Nevada State Prison. It was now highly effective, she said, but exorbitantly expensive, and treatment in the prison probably wouldn't be possible. She advised me that, after my release, I should see doctors on the outside.

The outside. The words were starting to resonate. It had been so long. For most of my life, I had known nothing besides steel bars, handcuffs, harsh words, and harsher acts. My very early years of growing up in Brooklyn, roaming about freely, driving my car as a teen—it all seemed like a dream. The outside? What would that even be like? My family was gone. My mother was dead, my father was dead, and though my dad's third wife had promised to take me in if I ever got out, she was also now deceased. The only one left was my sister, Marie, whom I hadn't spoken to in forty years. All she knew of me was what she'd read in the newspapers, that I had become a frightening, violent person. I hoped for the chance to sit down and talk to my sister. I wanted that chance. I hoped I could talk to Marie.

Although I was doing so much better than in the early days after my release from solitary, I still faced tough moments, especially in the culinary, a big open space crowded with convicts. My stomach tightened when I walked in. But I had developed a coping strategy. I would take my tray and lean against a wall, standing up while I ate. That way I could anticipate an anxiety attack and make a beeline for the exit if need be. But my plan fell apart when a guard shouted at me, "Sit down or get out!"

I tried to explain that I suffered from anxiety and needed to stand, but he wasn't hearing it. "I said, sit down or put the tray down and get out!"

I put the tray down and left. Fortunately, some of the cons snuck food out for me, and that's basically how I managed to eat.

In the back of my mind was always the fear of a much bigger setback, of a return to a catatonic state, to insanity. Many people in solitary go mad and never recover. Others commit suicide. I always remembered a guy named Robert Tostem. He was the guy I had been fighting in the bullpen when I was hit with eleven rounds of birdshot. Though he and I were sworn enemies, from a distance, I observed in him a confident tough swagger and an easy way. But years later, at Ely, before my own solitary nightmare had begun, I saw him being escorted to the infirmary. I stood still, barely recognizing him. He was being propped up by guards, making loud guttural sounds, his eyes roving around madly. He'd been in solitary for ten years. A few months later, he was dead. I was told he swallowed all his psych pills and chased them down with scouring cleanser and a bar of soap that he apparently choked on. That terrible image of him, enemy or not, is one I could never shake.

Though I bore deep scars, I knew I was one of the luckier ones. For inexplicable reasons, I came back from years in a catatonic state. I wasn't the same man I'd been before. Though I couldn't exactly put my finger on it, there were parts of me that were missing. Nonetheless, I did reconnect with reality, painful as that reconnection had been. But many others who've been driven mad in solitary do not return. My sanity was something I could never take for granted. If, for some reason, I disconnected again and was lost forever, I felt a pressing need to write something about my life. In the evenings, I sat in my cell, took pen to paper, and started with my boyhood in Brooklyn. I could practically smell the salt air of Coney Island. It felt so good. I recalled my painful family life and the love I felt for my parents, nonetheless. And, of course, I could never forget that moment when I was eleven and was being chased by that Shamrock bully who was ordering me to keep running or he'd kill me and how I'd turned the tables on him, never to run away again. I wrote about Vivien, my one and only love. Though it seemed like a lifetime since I'd bade her goodbye in the Nevada State Prison visit house, I'd never forgotten her. I put the pen down and blew her a kiss, hoping she'd had a happy life.

One afternoon, I was in the hall when I spotted none other than Chaplain James Stogner, who had visited me in solitary, the man who had called me his friend. He always wore a rather distinctive hat, and we'd had a little running banter about it. "I want my hat," I would tease. And now, here he was, standing in a hall at the Northern Nevada Correctional Center, wearing the same type of hat. He had not noticed me, so I crept up behind him and, in a low voice, said, "I want my hat."

He froze. "Huh? Frank? Is that you? Frank De Palma?!" Then he turned around. "Oh my God! I can't believe it!" he cried. "I can't believe it's you! Frank! Frank! How are you? I visited you in solitary, but it reached a point where you didn't recognize me anymore. I came to your cell window, banged on the door, but you never even knew I was there. You were crumpled over in pain, and you didn't seem to hear me or see me, and I couldn't get your attention. I would go back to my office and weep because you were gone. I feared my friend Frank would soon be dead. Oh, Frank, I'm so happy to see you! I'm so happy. Oh, thank you, God!"

Though physical contact between prisoners and civilians was strictly prohibited, he pulled me into a great bear hug anyway, and I hugged him back hard. As my friend and I laughed and cried, the guards looked the other way. My reunion with Chaplain Stogner remains one of my most precious moments.

Another prisoner, a pal named Richard Carmichael, also told me that he'd snuck into the solitary unit to see me but that

I hadn't responded to him either. "I could see you through the window," he said, "just sitting there, staring. I banged on the door, yelling 'Frank!' but there was absolutely no reaction from you. Nothing. You just sat there and stared straight ahead."

I shook my head as I heard these stories. I'd had no idea anyone had visited me. I'd been so far gone. Years and years were a total blank. I wish I had known there were people who cared about me. I'd felt so alone, and it would have meant so much. But learning about it now still made me feel good.

Following my encounter with Chaplain Stogner, another surprise encounter awaited. But this time, someone would recognize me, and I would be the one to freeze, trying to place the voice.

"Frank De Palma!" he shouted.

He sounded vaguely familiar, but nothing registered. I turned around to face an older Black convict, probably about my age. He flashed a broad smile. "You don't remember me?"

I shook my head. "No . . ."

"How about this: 'Where I come from, a handshake means something, even more than ink to paper.'"

"Oh! Oh my God . . ." And then it hit me. "Duke?!"

"Yeah, man, it's me, all right! It's been a while. Looks like we're both sporting a little gray," he joked.

I shook my head in disbelief, recalling my meeting with this man some twenty-five years earlier, just before the transfer to Ely. Duke, the head of the Black Mafia Family.

"Former head of the BMF," he said. "I'm not down with them anymore. Older, wiser, I guess. But I kept my word to you, didn't I?"

I nodded. "Yes, you did." This was the man who'd cancelled the orders to kill me, who'd turned off the deathly green light that had dominated so many years of my existence. Now, some twenty-five years later, he once again reached out to offer his hand. But instead of shaking, our arms opened instead, and we hugged each other, two old warriors who'd somehow survived.

After that, Duke and I became regulars on the yard. We lapped the perimeter each day, talking about things only the two of us could understand. Duke and I understood each other well. We'd fought the exact same war, the only thing separating us being our skin color. With the battles behind us, we could just be people now. Friends.

Duke worked in the kitchen and hooked me up with the biggest, juiciest cheeseburgers I'd ever tasted. A big old fat burger, lots of melted cheese, mayo, ketchup, thick slices of tomato, all piled high with fried onions. Heaven. He laughed so hard watching me devour it. This was the same guy who would have driven a knife into my chest at one time and to whom I would have returned the favor given the chance. Life is strange.

All in all, things were moving in a positive direction for me, which felt strange and unfamiliar. Regardless, I attributed it to Miss Walsh. She had become my treasured benefactor, a person who believed in me. So it was a hard day when I learned that she was being abruptly transferred from the Northern Nevada Correctional Center to another medium prison called Warm Springs. I did not get to speak with her before she left, and I feared I would never see her again. But I'd always made a point of thanking her for all she'd done for me. I hoped she truly understood just how grateful I was.

But my own stay at the Northern Nevada Correctional Center was also coming to a close. One morning, while I was out watering the garden, I was having a problem with the spigot. The new associate warden happened by, and I politely told him about the problem. But before I could finish, he interrupted me, "Your lifeline's gone, De Palma, she's gone. And now you're going to be gone too."

If the news that I was to be released from prison was a surprise to me, it stunned prison officials, who never could have imagined the day would come that Frank De Palma would be set free. Warden E.K. McDaniel's words summed it up: "Only two ways you're coming out of this cell—either you get released from prison, *and we both know that'll never happen . . .*" But now, it was happening, and the powers that be were none too pleased about it. If they couldn't block my release, then they would make my life as miserable as possible while they still could. I suspect their hope was to trip me up on another charge, thus ending any talk of release for good.

A couple of days later, I was packed up and bussed to the Lovelock Correctional Center, where I was thrown right back into solitary confinement. No explanation. After all those months on the Northern Nevada Correctional Center psych unit supposedly to help me recover from decades in isolation, here I was, right back in a lone cell. It was all very confusing. At first, I hung on to the progress I'd made. I went back to pacing, push-ups, and thinking of Miss Walsh, imagining her words of encouragement. But after a couple of months, I could no longer sustain it. Without even realizing it, I was fading away, merging with the walls, reconnecting with nothingness. But before I was completely lost, I took a chance and sent off a kite to Miss Walsh at Warm Springs. I hoped she would get it.

After six months at Lovelock, plans were in motion for me to be shipped back to Ely and returned directly to my solitary confinement cell. Nothing surprised me. Even after twenty-two years and thirty-six days in that cell, certain prison officials' anger toward me was as alive as ever.

But by some miracle, Miss Walsh got the kite. The morning I was to be loaded onto the bus for Ely, I was told the transfer had been blocked by the Inspector General's office. The IG is the arm of the Nevada Department of Prisons with ultimate authority over day-to-day operations. Apparently, an IG hold had been placed on the move. I didn't know what was happening behind the scenes, but next thing I knew, instead of Ely, I was on a bus bound for Warm Springs. My head was spinning.

CHAPTER 28

Looking Forward, Tentatively

The Inspector General was a man named Charles Evans. Once I was safely ensconced at the Warm Springs Correctional Center, I met him through a phone call in what turned out to be a warm and positive conversation. He said he was learning all about me, especially about my time in solitary. He urged me to take advantage of the many programs Warm Springs had to offer. He said he'd be keeping tabs on me and emphasized that he wanted me to be a good neighbor once I was released from prison.

I sensed I had another ally in Charles Evans, and I wanted to be a good neighbor, too. But honestly, I was still skeptical about a release. It was more like an abstract concept than anything else. Even if it was true, as everyone was saying it was, my entire life had been a series of deep and bitter disappointments. Someone had once told me I was the personification of Murphy's Law—anything that can go wrong will go wrong. I thought that about summed it up. Why would this be different?

Even though I had my doubts, I did have to admit that things felt different. The difference, of course, was Miss Walsh. Charles Evans never mentioned how I had come to his attention, but just like everything good that seemed to be coming my way, I assumed she had a hand in it. And the very best part of my transfer to Warm Springs was that I would be reunited with her.

But there was little time for sentimentality. By now, I was about two years away from my June 21, 2018, release date, and things were moving into the planning phase. A condition of my parole was that I was to be released to a halfway house, where I would live for six months. Miss Walsh was working on lining it up. If I wasn't convinced I was leaving, she certainly was.

For my part, she wanted me to be as prepared as possible for life on the outside. Since I had dropped out of high school, she said it was important I get my GED and my high school diploma.

"Both?!"

"Yes," she said. "You'll need every edge you can get."

By now, I knew better than to argue with her.

My first day in the classroom, which was located inside the prison compound, did not go well. The teacher chewed out a guy who was having trouble understanding something. This bothered me deeply. I wanted no part of this, so I got up and walked out.

Shortly afterward, I was in the yard when Miss Walsh caught up with me. "De Palma! I have a bone to pick with you. I enrolled you in school and I get a phone call telling me that ten minutes into your first class you get up and walk out. I am going to reenroll you and you will get your GED, and you will get your high school diploma!"

I tried to explain to her that my moral compass would not allow me to sit in a classroom with a teacher like that, but she was having none of it. "You get back in that classroom, and I don't want to hear another word about this. Do you understand?"

"Yes, ma'am!"

I returned to class and settled down to some serious studying—no easy task for a man who was not only sixty years old but whose brain did not function the way it had prior to solitary confinement. But the thought of letting Miss Walsh down was enough for me to push myself, sometimes putting in sixteen hours a day into study. For the first series of tests, the best I could do was a C minus. This did not satisfy me, and I dug in harder, working up to my first A. It was in English. It was a great feeling, a victory.

When I wasn't hitting the books, I was out in the yard every chance I had. If my tier hadn't been called and it was not my turn to go outside, I would sneak out anyway. But of course, Miss Walsh caught me. "De Palma! What are you doing out in the yard? You know you're not supposed to be out here now."

As wonderful as this woman was, she could also be a real pain in the ass.

"I know, Miss Walsh, but the allure of sunshine on my face after so many years of darkness . . . it's just too much sometimes."

For once, her face softened. "Yeah, I know, but I just don't want anything to trip you up at this point."

And I didn't want anything to trip me up either, so I followed the yard rules, avoided trouble, and focused on my schoolwork.

One afternoon, after I'd finished classes for the day, I was called to the infirmary. The doctor sat me down with some good news. He told me that every year, the prison chose a few people with a hepatitis diagnosis and provided their treatment. It entailed an eight-week regimen with a daily pill called Epclusa. He said he'd been going through my chart and that I qualified for it. I was thrilled. Over the next eight weeks, I faithfully took that pill. At the end, I was retested for hepatitis C and learned that, all these decades later, my body was finally free of the virus. Although my liver had been damaged, any further damage was halted. I always wondered if Miss Walsh had a part in my selection for this expensive treatment.

After months of slaving over the books, I passed my tests and received both my GED and high school diploma. I so wanted to make Miss Walsh proud, but I have to admit feeling a little proud of myself, too.

The completion of my schoolwork coincided with the announcement of a prison writing contest. Four winners would be selected. Spurred on by my classroom success, I entered the contest. The topic I chose was an overview of my forty-plus years in prison and the unique perspective it gave me, something even criminal justice experts can never truly understand. When the winners' list was posted, I was thrilled to see my name among the four. Another victory!

With school and the contest behind me, I got back to my own writing, picking up with my arrival at the Nevada State Prison at eighteen years old, well remembering my first sight of the place, and how scared I'd been, but also how hopeful I had been that I'd be home in two years. And then, of course, there was the burning memory of that pivotal yard meeting with Aryan Warrior leader Pat McKenna and my refusal to join his band. (As for McKenna, while I was preparing to leave prison, he was sitting on death row, awaiting execution.)

I reflected about how I'd changed from an everyday teen to a stone-cold predator and how quickly it had happened. I was just twenty-four years old during the max housing takeover and was already a dangerous young man. But so much had already happened to me. I'd been tortured by prison officials—chemically lobotomized and four-pointed underneath a bunk for three weeks. I don't know how I survived it. And then on the prisoner front, I'd faced years of deadly knife battles with the BMF. I recalled Copper Slim and Knuckles and how I'd fought off their rape attempt and of being presented with two sheets of steel afterward by an Aryan soldier. Old Folks had asked, "Are you a sheep or a wolf?" and I'd chosen wolf. There was no other way for me.

My decisions had kept me alive, but at what cost? When I'd first entered prison, I vowed I'd never become one of those black-hearted monsters who walked the yard. Yet in the end, I became one of the worst of them. As the fighting intensified and new charges piled up, my rage grew. During the max housing takeover with Bang-Bang, I'd held a gun in my hand, contemplating using it. It was such a crazy time. I smiled at the memory of Bang-Bang. In the prison environment, where kindness and compassion are considered weakness, and where feelings of friendship and love are to be viewed with suspicion and distrust, David "Bang-Bang" Wayne grew to become one of the few that I truly liked and respected. He was gone now, dying of cancer before he ever made it out. He was the last person to be buried in the convict cemetery located in a hilly area that separates the old women's prison from the now-retired Nevada State Prison. I hoped his spirit was at peace.

Out in the yard, I continued to attract attention, not only for my violent reputation but for the length of time I'd been locked up. One young gangbanger, a kid named Diablo, suggested I write about my life. "You should talk about back in the day, man. You lived it all! Your life is like a movie. Why don't you tell the mothers of these guys who come in here what's really happening to their sons? Why don't you go out there and be our voice? Why don't you write a book."

I felt a flash of irritation and batted him away. But he kept at it, urging me to write my whole story. I told him I'd think about it, more to get rid of him than anything else.

As I continued writing, my reflections grew deeper. I tried to understand how it could be that a teen who'd made a rash move when his dog was run over could have spent most of his life in prison as a result. I would never understand it.

Looking back, my life behind bars was roughly divided into two parts—equally horrible, just in different ways. The first was my war with the BMF. For almost two decades, I was thrust into dozens of knife fights with them. And though I'd survived, I'd taken someone else's life—Glen Stewart's. I didn't think of him often, but when I did, I could still hear his dying words: "They told me to get you." The scar on my shoulder was a lifelong reminder of that horrible morning—a morning I wish had never happened.

Just as my decades-long battle with the BMF finally ended with that handshake with Duke, part two began—solitary confinement. There were no words I could put to paper that could begin to capture the horror of prolonged isolation. It is a torture like none other, and I shuddered to think of the poor souls still in there. And, of course, I could never forget the singular event that led up to my punishment—my attempt to kill Sergeant Hogan. I could still picture the moment I'd tossed that chain around his neck, feeling completely justified in doing so. It was as though my attempt to kill him had come from the very depths of righteousness. For his part, I later learned that, years into my solitary stint, he was fired. I guess his dirty dealings finally caught up with him. Regardless of his actions toward me, I had no right to try to kill him. At the time, I'd felt otherwise. Now, I shake my head at how warped my thinking had become.

But in my own defense, the years of being immersed in violence, of expecting to die every single day, does something to a person. You can't exist in an abnormal environment without becoming abnormal, yourself. It was as though I existed in a dark, hate-infused dome with nothing good, warm, or loving to ever balance it out. Without the normal spectrum of human expression, one's sensibilities are distorted. I adapted to it, and I adapted very well.

Now that I was older and in the relatively gentler environs of Warm Springs, I could see things more clearly. When I had been in the midst of it, I couldn't. Although I confess to having done some bad things, I don't believe I was ever truly a bad person. In the end, I was very glad they had pulled me off Sergeant Hogan, and that the man had not died.

CHAPTER 29

The Wide Nevada Sky

With one year to go before my release, Miss Walsh was having no luck finding a halfway house that would accept me. I guess with a record of murder, attempted murder, assorted battery charges, and over forty years of incarceration, I did not make an attractive halfway house candidate. As the rejections piled up, I was glad I hadn't put a lot of stock into release. I could see another big letdown on the horizon. But then again, I also knew better than to discount the determination of one Lisa Walsh.

Halfway house or not, my time at Warm Springs was coming to a close. Both Miss Walsh and I would be leaving, but to different facilities. She was returning to the Northern Nevada Correctional Center, and I was being transferred to the Southern Desert Correctional Center for what was supposed to be my last year in prison. Although this separation would be final, she promised to keep working on the halfway house. We would communicate interdepartmentally.

Although Miss Walsh was still solidly behind me, as determined as ever that I make it out, other forces were at work, forces that were equally determined that I never saw the light of day. Though the plan to ship me back to Ely had been thwarted, they would try again.

I'd been told the reason I was leaving Warm Springs for Southern Desert was because it was reportedly a premier program facility—one of the best in the state! It was touted for its various reentry programs, which would give me greater tools for making it on the outside. It sounded like a logical next step, and I was hopeful about this transfer.

Yet the day I arrived, I could see it was nothing but hype. Far from a rehabilitative atmosphere, Southern Desert was a zoo—a gang stronghold and an open market for crack cocaine, meth, and heroin, the likes of which rivaled the yard at the Nevada State Prison. And even if there were any useful programs, it hardly mattered as they had me locked down in a cell every other day. I had the distinct feeling that, by being sent here, I'd been set up. Among other things, this place was a gladiator school, and I suspected the hope was that I'd get caught up on another charge and they could "cross me out," meaning I would never leave.

But I wasn't taking the bait. I stayed in my cell, and on the days I was on the yard, I was cautious. There were some tense moments, but I got through them. As I resisted getting pulled into the fray and with my release date drawing closer, some of the guards became hostile, laughing in my face at my prospect of freedom. "Hey, De Palma, how long you think you'll last out there? A week—two weeks? Ha, ha, ha!" They started openly taking wagers on it. They weren't betting on whether I'd come back to prison; that was a foregone conclusion. They were betting on how long I'd last.

But I didn't care. They could laugh all they wanted. I was on a mission now. The big factors, as always, were Miss Walsh and Charles Evans, but especially Miss Walsh. After all she'd done for me, I could not let her down. But I also didn't want to let myself down. I was ready to move on in every way. I'd been to hell and back, and I knew this was my chance—a real chance. Walsh's and Evans's dream for my release was my dream now. I wanted to leave, and I thought about it all the time. I'd be sixty-two when I got out. Could I build a life for myself? Was it too late? I lay in my bunk at night, wondering what my life would have been had it unfolded normally. Would I have done something spectacular? Or would I have been an average Joe? I would never know. But with what little time I had left, I still hoped to make something of it.

Of course, everything hinged on the halfway house. Without it, I was going nowhere. My June 21st release date came and went. A letdown. But Miss Walsh remained determined.

On those days when I was out of my cell, the young kids kept coming up to me, just as they had at the Northern Nevada Correctional Center, asking this old man, "Are you Frank De Palma?"

"Yep, that's me," I said, and kept walking.

But one of them, no more than eighteen or nineteen years old, kept following me. I finally stopped and asked him what he wanted. He looked so young, and I must have appeared so old and scary to him. He told me he was here on a "nickel and dime" charge. He just wanted to do his time, about a year, and get out. But he said he was terrified, and that he was being propositioned by a gang. He didn't want to join, but he feared they'd hurt him if he refused. "Do you have any advice?" he asked me.

Of course, I saw my own face in his, remembering my same question of Pops way back in the beginning: "Do you have any advice for me?" I'd asked him.

My heart warmed. I would help this kid in any way I could. "Yes," I said. "I do have advice. First of all, don't join the gang. No matter what they tell you, they don't love you, and they're not your brothers. You will have to make your bones, which means violence, and that will lead to new charges that could keep you in here forever."

"Yeah, but if I tell them no, I'm afraid they're going to hurt me."

I nodded my understanding and suggested something very difficult, but something that I only wished had been in place and an option for me when I first came in. I advised him to go to the prison officials and tell them he wanted to be placed in protective custody. "You'll be alone in a cell with an hour a day out for rec, but it will end in a year. You'll also be out with others on the tier, so it's a little easier than solitary confinement."

He looked at me in disbelief.

"Like it or not, you don't have any other options," I told him. "Your life is on the line."

When we parted, I just hoped he would take me seriously.

A few days later, I passed an administrative office and saw him sitting inside, talking to a sergeant. I did a fist pump and smiled. *Yeah!* Maybe I'd made a difference.

Five months after my release date had come and gone, finally—good news! Miss Walsh had succeeded. I had been accepted to a halfway house in Reno. It was official. I now had a new release date: December 21, 2018.

My forty-three-year prison stint would end. I was soon to be a free man. I pinched myself. I would be on parole for the rest of my life, but still, I would experience life without handcuffs, leg irons, and chains. I lay on my bunk at night, trying to imagine it.

For a lifetime spent in what felt like torturous slow motion, the remaining months sped by. On the day before my release, I was to be bussed from Southern Desert to Warm Springs, where I would spend the night before being set free from that facility the following morning. But for some inexplicable reason, I was placed on the wrong bus. Instead of Warm Springs, the bus was destined for Ely State Prison, of all places. I would have to stay at Ely overnight before an early morning bus trip back to Warm Springs for release.

It had been four years since I'd hobbled out of that solitary cell at Ely, and as the van pulled up to its gates, my stomach lurched. Inside, I recognized many of the guards, most of them shocked to learn I was being released. A few wished me well, while others started up on the wagering, betting how long I'd make it on the outside.

But my mind was elsewhere. This unexpected detour to Ely gave me an opportunity to take care of a little business. While they joked around, I asked a favor. "Take me up to death row."

"Awhh, come on, De Palma, what do you want to go up there for?"

"It'll only take a few minutes."

They groaned but honored my final request, escorting me to the somber unit. As we passed by the cell doors, familiar faces were in the windows, shouting, "Frankie! Is that you? Hey! Franko!"

I waved to them all.

Then I found the cell I was looking for and the person I wished to speak with. He was wearing a headset, tapping his foot to music.

I tapped the window. "Hey, Pat."

Pat McKenna, the once feared Aryan Warrior leader, pulled off the headset and drew back at the sight of me. Though we were both old men now, we recognized each other instantly. His curly brown hair was gray, his face drawn and wrinkled. He no longer looked scary, just old and tired.

"What are you doing here?" he demanded.

"Hey, Pat, you remember those four dudes who tried to rape me when I first came in?"

"I don't know what you're talking about."

"You were behind it. I know you were. Everybody knows it. You set it up so I'd get raped and then killed. All because I had the nerve to refuse your invitation. But it didn't work, Pat. It didn't work. And now I'm getting out of prison. Yup, that's right. I'm going home tomorrow."

"Just what do you think's out there for you?" he sneered.

"I don't know, but I'm going to find out—something you'll never have a chance to do. You're staying right here on death row, and here's where you're going to die."

He batted his hand at me and pulled his headset back on.

I walked away. I'd said my piece.

Around two in the morning, I was awakened for the ride back to Warm Springs. It was about a five-hour drive. I stayed awake the entire time, watching the sky as it slowly lightened, a new day dawning on the horizon. I couldn't help but notice how majestic the sunrise looked, in much the same way it had looked some forty-three years earlier when a scared, freckle-faced kid had been driven to the Nevada State Prison. I'd come into prison a young man, my life ahead of me; now, I was leaving an old man, my life behind me.

Back at Warm Springs, everything moved quickly. I traded in my oranges for civilian clothes and was handed twenty-five dollars that I tucked in my pocket. A van would meet me outside the visit area to take me to the halfway house. As I walked into the visit room, wearing jeans, a flannel shirt, and a jacket, and mingling with the visitors, it finally became real. I was one of them. The guards looked on impassively as I got on the line waiting to exit the facility.

When the door opened, I stepped out and beheld the wide-open Nevada sky. A free man, at last.

THE END

Epilogue

America is the land of the second chance—and when the gates of the prison open, the path ahead should lead to a better life.
—GEORGE W. BUSH

On December 21, 2018, at the age of sixty-two, Frank De Palma left prison. In the forty-three years that he had been behind bars, beginning when he was just eighteen, the world had changed dramatically. With his parents deceased and most family long gone, Frank faced an unfamiliar world alone. After several months at a halfway house, he was released to homelessness. Determined to fight the odds that he'd never make it on the outside, he sat upright on park benches through frigid winter nights, fearful that lying down to sleep would attract the attention of police. With the assistance of ex-cons, he was directed to soup kitchens and to the few support services available to the homeless.

Despite his dire straits, Frank greeted strangers and new friends with a smile, determined to experience the flip side of his hate-filled prison years—the side of joy, friendliness, laughter, and warmth. To every person he met, he also told them about his prison life and his years in solitary. Coincidentally, Frank's release came at a moment of growing public recognition of the horror of solitary confinement, and the Nevada legislature was considering reforms to the brutal practice. At the request of the

Nevada ACLU, on March 26, 2021, Frank testified before the Nevada Senate Judiciary Committee, describing his staggering twenty-two years and thirty-six days in isolation. When he was finished, there was a stunned silence before Chairwoman Melanie Scheible said, "In the work that we do, there are a few days that you will never forget; speaking for myself, this is one of them. Hearing your story will never leave me."

As Frank struggled to survive, his advanced age and the years of hard living were taking their toll, and his body was failing. He was hospitalized with congestive heart failure, which was just the beginning of a litany of serious medical conditions he would face. And with every x-ray taken, doctors were shocked at the amount of birdshot lodged inside his body.

When a debilitating spinal issue left Frank in a wheelchair, he lived in a day motel, getting by on a disability check and GoFundMe contributions. But he had hope. There was the promise of a surgery that would restore his ability to walk and a growing sense of a larger purpose. During his legislative testimony, he met Mary Buser, author of *Lockdown on Rikers: Shocking Stories of Abuse and Injustice at New York's Notorious Jail*, and a former assistant chief of mental health at New York City's Rikers Island, who had also testified before the Nevada judiciary. As they became acquainted, he told her about his writings and his nagging memory of fellow convict, Diablo, who had urged him to write about his life. "Why don't you go out there and be our voice?" Diablo had said.

Frank started to feel that this was his mission, and he and Mary began collaborating on a book. As Frank recounted the details of his life, he became ever more determined to shine a light on the cut-off world of prisons, to speak for the voiceless, forgotten masses inside, and especially for "the forgotten of the forgotten"— the thousands still existing in solitary confinement.

Thankfully, Frank's spinal surgery was successful, and he was once again able to walk. On another good note, Frank's dream of reconnecting with his sister was realized. After decades of estrangement, he finally had that chance to sit down with Marie and tell her everything that had happened. To this day, he and his sister remain in close touch.

As Frank strives to get on with his life, reforms have come about in the Nevada prison system. In 2016, the use of birdshot was discontinued. In terms of solitary confinement, despite Frank's compelling testimony in 2021, the bill languished. But, in 2023, the effort was revived, in the form of Bill SB307, which would place substantial constraints on the use of solitary confinement in Nevada's prison system. On June 15, 2023, Governor Joseph Lombardo signed it into law. With this victory, current and future prisoners will never be subjected to the torture that Frank De Palma and so many others have endured.

Acknowledgments

To Marie and Steve Padilla, for teaching me that love isn't earned, it's given. But mostly, thank you for "enduring me."

To the memory of my baby sister, Jackie. I never grieved for you because the pain runs too deep. But I'll never forget you and will always love you. Your big brother, Frankie.

Richard Carmichael, what can I say? You've become my brother, my best friend, and I love you with my life. Thanks for everything.

Nick Shepack and Bradlyn Wissert, thank you for being such loyal friends, and for always being there for me. I hold you both close to my heart, and that's forever. Thank you.

Jessica Taylor, my life has been filled with extreme and intense experiences, most of them bad, but since I met you, you've made so many of the demons that haunt me fade away. Thank you for the gift of you.

To Kathleen Fogarty, thank you for remembering and caring about what happened to me and to three other lowly prisoners some forty years ago, and for fighting for prisoners' rights back then—and to this day. I'm so grateful for you.

Dr. Richard Price, thank you for making me walk again, and perhaps equally important, for not giving up on me. Thank you.

To Martin Wiener, my attorney who defended me at my murder trial. I want to thank you for believing me—it meant so very much to be believed. Thank you, Mr. Wiener, for fighting for me.

To Chaplain James Stogner—you touched my heart when I learned you cried for me when I was in solitary. Thank you for calling me your friend.

Thank you, former Associate Warden, Lisa Walsh—you are the reason I didn't sabotage myself. If it wasn't for you, I never would have made it out. I am forever indebted to you.

Rod Moore—thanks for everything, and especially for being a friend and not a cop!

To Dr. Nathaniel Woods, the only psych I spoke with after I got out of solitary who "got me" and who I felt comfortable with. Thank you for being there for me, Dr. Woods.

Senior C.O. Todd Miller, you believed in me from the very beginning, which helped me to continue on. I'll never forget you. Thank you.

To Angela Hattery and Earl Smith—my two happy people and my biggest advocates. Thank you for rooting for me, for supporting me, and for being such good friends. Love you both!

Holly Welborn, I want to thank you for taking up my cause and making it personal. I also want to thank you for the birthday party you threw for me—it was the best one ever!

Lacy Foster and Nikki Foster, thank you for all your kind help and friendship. I shall cherish you both forever.

Elaine Voight, thank you for being an ally and friend, and for getting me to my appointments, and helping me out in so many ways. And thanks to your son, Tony, also for helping me out and for being a friend. Rest in peace, Tony.

Thank you to Ash Jones for always believing in me and pushing me to get the book done.

Thomas Freeme, thank you for motivating me and for being a good friend.

Jim Firewalker, thank you for being a friend and for all the hopeful insight you gave me.

To Mark Spadt, I have a small circle of those I care about,

and you are one of them. I want to thank you for teaching me to be around people again. It was hard but you stuck with me, and I'm forever grateful. Thank you, brother. I love you.

Thank you, Haywood Wilson, for the smile you put on my face the first day I was out. You're a good friend.

Big Rob—brother, you never cease to embarrass me with all the praise you bestow upon me but thank you for being a friend because they are few and far between.

To Daniel Tiberio (aka Boston), thank you for calling my name when I was homeless. You got me off the streets. I'll never forget you, my friend.

Raymond Mascarenas, you had my heart the day I got out and you were there waiting for me, just like you said you would.

To Michael Mercado, my best iron pile workout partner, and all-around good friend. Long live the Gobbagucci Brothers!

Thank you, Stephanie Johnson, and everyone at Stepping Stones; to Jessica Leech, who's been like a little sister, to Mera Mehta, for being a very special woman; to Shawna Silva at HOPES for finding my writings, and to Nicole, my therapist for a time—I enjoyed our conversations.

To "Social Workers & Allies against Solitary Confinement," thank you for welcoming me into your circle and supporting me so vigorously. You are a source of inspiration and motivation.

Thank you, Sandy Bernabei. I so admire your "get it done" mentality. The hell with the red tape —let's get it done!

To April Strommer, for all your help with my website. Thank you, April!

To Ali Winters, I love your spirit! You're awesome. Can't wait to hang out with you!

To everyone who's done time and looked out for me when I got out, thank you. I wouldn't have made it without you.

A huge thank-you to those who contributed to the

GoFundMe! Your generosity and your love carried me through some very dark moments. Bless you!

A special thank-you to those who read the manuscript: Anne Ashley Quinn, Thomas Buser, Kathleen Fogarty, Karen A. Cassidy, Bettina Faltermeier, Wolfgang Demisch, and Mary Lou Buser. For your time, interest, and feedback, I am deeply grateful to all of you.

For their wonderful work on the book, thank you to editor Michele Matrisciani, cover designer Zarah Zurita, copyeditor Carol Rosenberg, book designer Gary Rosenberg, and Lloyd Jassin, Esq.

Finally, I wish to acknowledge Mary Buser, my book collaborator, confidante, and dear friend. You came into my life and enriched it beyond my wildest dreams. Thank you, and I love you forever.

And thanks to Fatty, my big fat cat, who's brought tranquility into my life.

About the Authors

Frank De Palma was incarcerated for forty-three years in the Nevada prison system, for an initial nonviolent charge. During this time, he was held in solitary confinement at Ely State Prison for twenty-two years and thirty-six days. Since his release in 2018, he has advocated for the abolition of solitary confinement and for humane treatment of prisoners. In March 2021, he testified before the Nevada Senate Judiciary Committee about his experience in solitary. He has been featured in numerous articles, including "The Marshall Project" "Solitary Watch", and has appeared in short films about solitary confinement produced by Al Jazeera and the Irish film production company, Wonderbread. Frank lives in Reno, Nevada, with his little cat, Fatty.

Mary Buser is an award-winning author of *Lockdown on Rikers: Shocking Stories of Abuse and Injustice at New York's Notorious Jail,* based on her work in the Rikers Island mental health department. An advocate for criminal justice reform, she is Codirector of Social Workers & Allies against Solitary Confinement, and has written numerous articles, appearing in *The Washington Post, The Daily Beast, Politico,* and *New York Daily News.* Mary lives in Brooklyn, New York.